VITALITY
— HANNA ABI AKL —

Vitality
Copyright © 2018 by Hanna Abi Akl
Waterton Publishing Company

All rights reserved. No part of this book may be reproduced, stored, or transmitted by any means—whether auditory, graphic, mechanical, or electronic—without written permission of the author, except in the case of brief excerpts used in critical articles and reviews. Unauthorized reproduction of any part of this work is illegal and is punishable by law.

Because of the dynamic nature of the Internet, any web addresses or links contained in this book may have changed since publication and may no longer be valid. The views expressed in this work are solely those of the author and do not necessarily reflect the views of the publisher, and the publisher hereby disclaims any responsibility for them.

ISBN 978-0-9905249-8-4

watertonpublishing.com

Contents

Loss	9
Reprise	10
Rudimentary	14
Possibly	15
Cold fusion	18
Nebula	20
End of the line	22
Don't worry, kid	23
A song	25
Unknown streets	26
On the clock	27
Good word	30
Your lap	32
Chapter	33
Interruptions	36
Genuine contact	38
Greatness	39
Midnight in Paris	40
The shells of life	42
Legacy	43
Correlation	45
Foam	47
The cruelest fate	49
Dark Corners	50
Wherever she is	52
Oddity	55

VITALITY

Rain-man	56
Testimony	60
To this day	61
The human race	62
The finishing line	63
Spikes	68
2/9/2018	71
Unfinished hearts	73
Sequence	74
How long	77
We are	78
No matter	79
Freight Train	81
Observation	87
When	92
Basic need	95
Insanity	97
Overshoot	99
Little girl with dark eyes	100
Some dream	102
In this city	104
Crawl	105
Fallout	108
Killing softly	109
Blame	110
Destined	111
No more lines	113
Final letter	117

Infinite *121*
Little fears *122*
Creation *127*
Remember me *129*
Peaches for my roses *131*
Caught inside a dream *138*
The move *141*
I seldom read the writers *144*
Decisive People *146*
Influence *147*
The writing process *149*
The things she likes *151*
Wonderwall *154*
To this life *157*
Hidden world *158*
Letter One *160*
Vedette *163*
Same Ode *166*
Without Knowing *170*
I am the creator *173*
You can have your men *174*
Open your heart *176*
Travelers *178*
Bad days *180*
My being *181*
I don't miss anything *183*
Joy *185*
I walked from door to door *186*

VITALITY

Still writing at 80 .... *189*
The Open Road *191*
If they ask me for the truth *192*
I beat a man at the pool table *193*
Her *196*
Power cut *198*
The last time *200*
Visions *202*
Holy Trinity *204*
The thread *205*
Vitality *207*
To the women in this book *211*
Skyline *212*
Playing for keeps *214*
No good *215*
Sometimes *216*
The glass *218*
Half *220*
Heavy world *221*
The good lines *223*
Where do the masses go *226*
Today *228*
Fall back *230*
One morning *232*
Hands of love *233*
Ruminating *234*
Burning Desire *236*
Empire *237*

There is a light inside you *239*
Never call yourself a writer *241*
Different Universes *242*
After me *244*
Banners *246*
My poetry *247*
Run script *249*
Defining people *251*
It takes a few words *253*
These words are a book *256*
Rules *257*
Stage name *258*
If she reads this *260*
Turns *265*
Implosion *267*
I find it insane *268*
The road to you *269*
Poetic Reasoning *271*
I made a deal with god *272*
Read these lines *274*
The devils are here *275*
Numbers *278*
Stop *280*
Madness *283*
Traces *286*
In any act of creation *289*
As simply as I can *292*
Still *295*

Venture by the Sea *299*
Passing in front of the small humble place *301*
Backdoor *303*
Pipe dream *305*
Places *306*
Light-Bringer *307*
Wonder *310*
Rubble *311*
Revival *314*
Passion on paper *316*
Toast *319*
A light *320*
I lent her my heart *321*
We forget to feel *324*
Breathing you *327*
Luck of the word *329*
Mockingbird *331*
Salvation *333*
World view *336*
Don't go looking for heroes *338*
Still-frame *340*
Signs of love *343*
Yellow Flower *345*
Coffee Lady *347*
Regression *350*
Ode to the Storm *353*
Crossing over to you *356*
About the author *358*

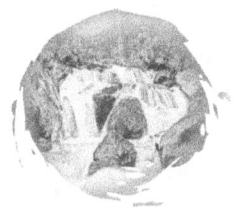

LOSS

I have always been
For the anti-hero
The man with a dark side
The lone wolf
Who answers with a shrug
Of the shoulder

He who is capable
Of being a deserter
In an epic battle

A rescuer
In unexpected moments.

VITALITY

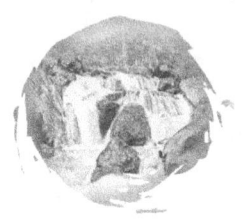

REPRISE

Here we go
Again
On another
Night
Thinking
About
Another life
And how much
Drinking
It will take
To forget
Or numb
Myself
To sleep

My gut
Wrenches
Like a sac
Full of stones

It weighs me
Down
And with it
My vision
My hearing
My taste
Are impaired

But the mind
The mind
Is always
Stronger
Rebellious
Defiant
It does not
Crumble
Under the quaking
Of rocks
It does not
Surrender
To the onslaught
Of the dead

And so
It begins
Again
Like a flow
From the gut
To the mouth

VITALITY

To the mind
To the eyes
Rainbows are
Drawn and
Quickly scraped;
Voices circle
In the room
And quickly dissipate
Into the thin cold
Walls

Where are they?
Where is she?
Where am I?

And the reigning
Silence
Is king;
It settles
Again
Reversing the
Aging of time
And bringing back
Painful memories:

We
Do
Not
Let
Go

Easily
Of those
We
Have once
Cared
About

And the silence
Remains

And the silence
Remains.

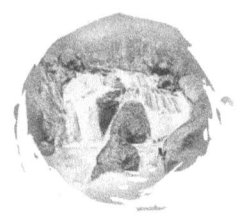

Rudimentary

Demented
Men
And
Enchanted
Spirits
Were always
Meant
For
Different
Worlds.

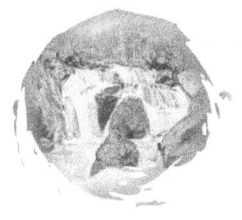

POSSIBLY

Possibly
I look at them
Sneering
Wondering
Why
I couldn't have
What they had:
A couple
Kissing
In the train
Station
His back
Against the wall
Her kisses
Engulfing his
Large neck
He holds her
Like he holds the moon
He grips her waist

VITALITY

Tightly
And cups it
Between his hands
His eyes
Never leaving me
Or any other human
Alone
As if
To mark
His territory
And protect
What is
His

Humans
Are strange
Creatures
They fight
And push each
Other away
Only to
Fiercely
Regroup
And defend
The same thing
They care about
But
I was
Past

That
I was past
The resignation
Of never obtaining
What I never really
Wanted
Or attempted
To seriously
Look for:
I paid
For
The ticket
Boarded
The train
Only
To realize
I was
Alone.

VITALITY

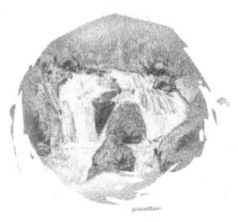

COLD FUSION

I have been
To the other
Side
And there is
Nothing
Glamorous
Or romantic
In riding trains
With strangers
Or walking past
A flock of pigeons
Eating breadcrumbs
Off the ground

Here the people
Lacked foresight:
They couldn't see
Through me

Imagine their
Shock
When they learned
Writers
Are the scientists
Of the
Unspoken world.

VITALITY

NEBULA

In these intense
Moments
Of reflection
You wait
For a
Nebula
Or some
Kind of
Truth
To hit you

But
It's just
A feeling
An eerie
Familiar
Feeling
You've been
Hiding from

Or pushing
Back
All along.

VITALITY

END OF THE LINE

End of the line
Turning the page
Closing yet
Another book

I decided
I wanted
Someone
Who would
Put up
For me
Half the fight
I did
For everybody else

And she
Was worth
Finding.

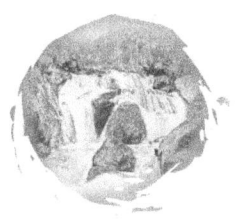

DONT WORRY, KID

Even the fridge
And the walls
And the windows
And the sink
Seemed to
Speak
Their noise
Filling in
The room
As if
They were
Telling me:
Don't worry,
Kid
Something
Good
Will come
Out
Of this –

VITALITY

There's
A good
Life
Waiting
For
You.

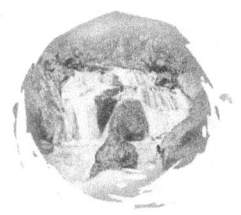

A SONG

She was
Like a song
Whose lyrics
You couldn't
Remember
Until it
Replayed
On the radio
And became
Increasingly
Difficult
To
Forget.

VITALITY

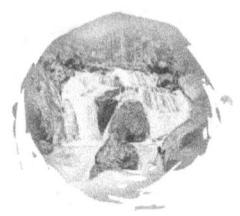

UNKNOWN STREETS

Walking down
Long distant
Streets
Where
People
Are looking
To be
Found
Or perhaps
Just
Understood.

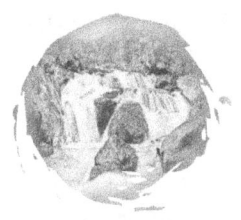

ON THE CLOCK

Remember?
Remember the way
She pointed
At the clock
Showing 11:11
Before she waved you off
And stepped out
Of the car
Leaving the door
Open
In the middle of a traffic
Jam.
Her hips
Strutting
On the sidewalk
While policemen
Gave her
All kinds of dirty
Looks

VITALITY

Through their shady
Sunglasses.
And you
Still driving
Ever at one
With the road
With the asphalt
Almost glued
At the steering
Wheel
Thinking
Of the open car door
That hasn't been closed
Thinking about
The dirty policemen
And law enforcers
Thinking about
The music
On the radio set
Thinking about
The burning sun
That left her face
The only thing
Untouched
By the heat.
Thinking about
The 11:11
And her words

Ringing
Among the car horns
The loud desperate noises
Of people
Who had never known
The beginning
Of love:
When in
Doubt,
Make a wish
On the 11:11.
Today
I am
The fool
Who still
Wishes
For her
On the clock.

GOOD WORD

Though little
Of it
Is on the
Surface
I still
Ask it
To please
Keep
Coming:
It is
The dividing
Tide
Between
How much
We want
Things
To be
Right
And how

Much
Of them
Really is.

VITALITY

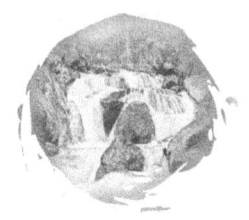

YOUR LAP

To rest
On your
Lap, still –
I am
Boarding
The plane
And only
One thing
Crosses
My mind:
To rest
My head
On
Your lap.

CHAPTER

Wherever
The start
Wherever
The end
For me
There is
Only
Now
The moment
The crossroads
The obelisk mounted
On the highest plain
The city
The airport
The people
Waving
Saying their goodbyes
And looming uncertainty

VITALITY

Whenever I play back
The steps
That got me
Here
I always
Fancy
My former-self:
Young
Reckless
Excited

Now the man
Writing the lines
Is grey-haired
Grey-hearted
Fearful
Of what is
To come;

The city
Has been good
To me
And I leave
It all
Behind me
Knowing
In my deepest thoughts
There are no
Regrets

This life
Is
Everything
And
The only thing
We've got
But it's worth
Living.

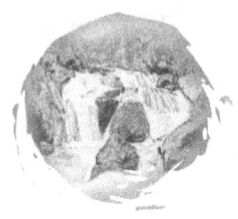

INTERRUPTIONS

Whether it's
Education
Career
Writing
Something
Always seems
To get
In the way
Of relationships;
When
Was it
Love's
Turn?
Interruptions
There were always
Interruptions
Or maybe
Vessels
To avoid

The loving
The women
The sweet talks
The dreamy gazes

The problem
Is that
Those
Who have
The ability
To love
Don't do
It
Properly.

VITALITY

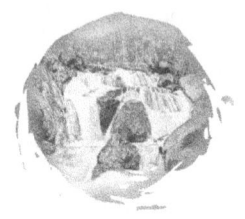

GENUINE CONTACT

I still
Believe
That
In this
Place
In this
World
Full
Of egos
And self-feeding
Minds
There is
Room
For
Raw emotion
And a deep
Connection
Of
The human soul.

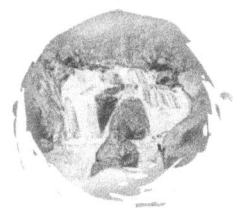

GREATNESS

The moment
We elevate
Others
And witness
Greatness
In them
Is
The start
Of our
Own
Downfall.

VITALITY

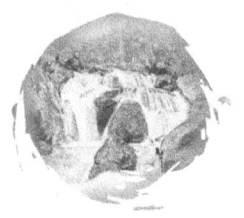

MIDNIGHT IN PARIS

Midnight in Paris –
As I sit alone
And think
Of her:
Where
Did
The
Hours
Go?
I could've
Been
A good
Lover;
No,
I could've
Been
A great
Lover
If not

For
This fragile
Heart
But I will
Avenge
The years
And I will
Find her
Among
The stars
Because
The love
I believe
In
Is
Transcendent:
It
Is
More
Than
This life,
It
Is
More
Than
Itself.

VITALITY

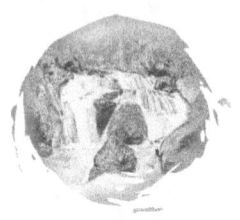

THE SHELLS OF LIFE

To walk upon
The shells
Of life
While avoiding
Judgment
Prejudice
Contempt
Is placed
Alongside
The greatest
Mysteries
Even the most
Resolute
Men
Have failed
To
Address.

LEGACY

I will keep
Writing
The books
I will
Keep
Writing
The mediocre books
Until they become
Great
Or at least
Good;
I will keep
Draining
The moments —
And if a few
Of them
Were to be
Great
Then I will

VITALITY

>
> Call them
> My
> Legacy.

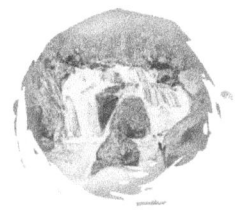

CORRELATION

After all
This time
I was finally
Able
To see
Her
For what
She
Truly was:
Human.
And in
The end
That was
The single
Trait
That granted us
The ability
To give
So much

VITALITY

> Love
> And
> Receive it.

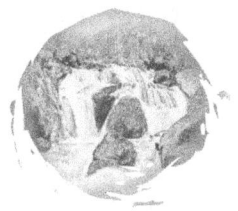

FOAM

When I was
A kid
My father
Used to
Tell me
To place
My hand
On my forehead
While washing
My hair
To shade my eyes
From
The foam.
Now
As
I am
Much older
I still
Do it

VITALITY

And eclipse
My eyes
From the foam
But with every
Passing day
A growing sensation
Tells me
Maybe
My father
Was trying
To protect
Me
From
Something
More.

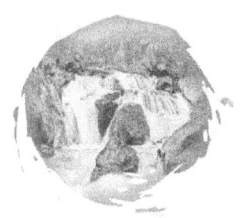

THE CRUELEST FATE

The cruelest
Fate
We can wish
Upon ourselves
Is believing
The people
We see
In a certain light
See us
The same
Way.

Vitality

Dark Corners

She
Told
Me:
You look
Like
Someone
In need
Of answers

Honey,
I write
The dirty
Way
I'm not afraid
Of going
Into the darkest
Corners
Of the
Word

And if
Seeking
Answers
Was ever
A mad
Endeavor
Then I don't
Want to be
Sane.

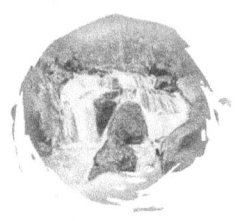

Wherever she is

Wherever
She is
Now
And if
She still
Pays attention
To
The little
Things like
The raindrops
The suffocation
Of the
Human soul
I would like
To let her
Know
She is
Still
With me

On every
Sleepless
Night
Inside
Every
Waking dream
Her features
Appear
In movies
Poetry
Artistic frivolous
Images
And when
I crack open
A window
Or light a small
Fire
I would like
To think
She is still
Somewhere
Near
In thought –
Perhaps
Even
Searching
Herself
For something

Vitality

That can't be
Explained
A rhythm
Or a line
Or a blank space

Darling,
My excavation
Has led me
To walk upon
These lines
So I am
Sending
Them
Your
Way.

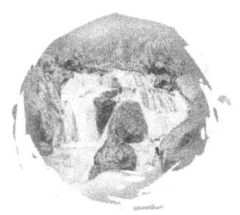

ODDITY

The oddity
Is that
I may wake up
One day
Feeling like
A groggy
Little dog
That has not yet
Been fed
And another
Like a
Miracle-god
Bemused
By the
Trials
Of the saints.

VITALITY

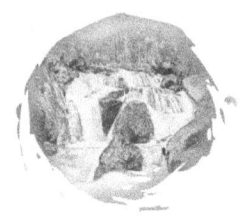

RAIN-MAN

He sits
In a small
Coffee shop
And types
His notes
His remarks
His observations

In front of him
The sickness
Rolls down
Every cheek
The anxiety
Spreads
In the air

He has developed
Some kind of
Immunity

To these things
And other
Things
Such as
Holding
Onto
A woman's
Hand
Or hanging out
With former friends
Now turned estranged
Immigrants

He watches
The world
Shift and change
Over the years
From the same spot
The same position
And the magnifying glass
That browses through life
Does not reach him;
He is sheltered
From it
Just like he is sheltered
Away from
The stares
And judgment
Of others.

VITALITY

He watches them
He watches all
And I watch
Him
But he doesn't
See me
Unaware
That another
Human being
Might possibly
Take interest
In him.

But I do not
Take interest
I take comfort;
I take comfort
In knowing
He is doing well
Holding up
On his own
Against the cruelty
And violence
And ferocity
Of the world
The rapid spins
And changes
That hit us
From all sides

I watch him
And I can read it
In his eyes
I can see
His eyes
Weighing down
On his notes
And asking
The same
Old
Question:
What will
It take
From civilization
To drag itself
Out of the rut
And step up?

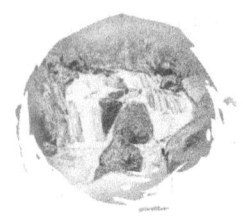

TESTIMONY

Going
Back and
Forth
Between
Here
And the valley
Of the dead
To seek
Hidden answers
To eternal
Questions

Or
You saying
White shoes
Are meant
To be
Worn
Dirty.

TO THIS DAY

To this day
I can still
Say with
Certitude,
I wrote
To
Save
My
Goddamn
Life.
And that
Has been
My
Greatest
Treasure.

THE HUMAN RACE

The fact that
Most people
Struggle to finish
A book
Nowadays
Should tell you
Enough
About
The human
Race.

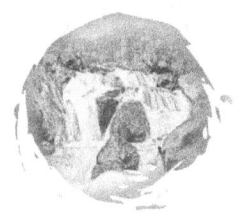

THE FINISHING LINE

It is
Right there
Chalk-marked
On the floor.
I crawl
Towards it:
Hesitant
Willing
Unwilling
The laughs break out
Around me
As I dodge
Spit missiles
Coming from
Every direction.
Yes,
I think,
Sometimes
It's better

Vitality

To be alone.
There are
Certain
Scenarios
Where it
Is
Always better
And advisable
To go
At
It
Alone;
To be
By yourself
And clear
The noise
Shake the disturbance
From
Your
God-given
Aura.
To touch
The line
Before
It erases
Itself
That
Was

My only
Wish
Should
I fail
To cross
It.
But worse men
Have managed
To make it
To the other
Side
And right now
I think,
Why
Not
Me
Then?
Maybe
I
Lacked
The spunk
The spine
To go
All the way
Down
The victory road
Paved with flame torches
Of fury and fame;

VITALITY

But as the resounding
Sounds
Of road blockers
Pull me
Back
Here I am
Now
Close to it:
Close to touching
The white line
Extending
From here
To there
My eyes
Unshifting
From the faded color
Sucked into
The grey
Asphalt
Unconcerned
Even
By what lies
Beyond
It;
To tell
You
I made it
Is not

The real
Story
Here
But to say
That I know
I am able
To get across
Should be a
Daunting thought
On its
Own.

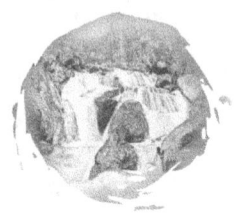

SPIKES

How many
Silences
Do we wish
We kept?

How many
Moments
Do we wish
We took back?

If the world
Around us
Is measured
In moments
How many
Of them
Are truly
Outstanding?

How many
Are undesirable?

How many
Are erasable?

To me
Life
Is not
Measured
In
Moments —

Rather
It is
Measured
In spikes:

Spikes of
Bliss
Spikes of
Fortune
Spikes of
Madness.

And on a day
Where the sun
Fused harmoniously
With a few sprinkles
Of rain

VITALITY

There was a single
Spike
I wished
To take back
From her;

A single
Moment
I wished
To retract
Or substitute.

How many of these
Lines
Ring true
In your thoughts
Just now?

How many such
Moments
Have presented themselves
With no
Prior notice

How many times
Have you thought about
A person
Just to have them
Reach out to you
Unexpectedly?

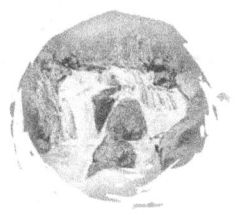

2/9/2018

And now
I've shed
My skin
I am
Naked –
Flesh
Mind
Soul –
But I still
Speak
To her
Intermittently
Through
My lines:
I'm still
Pulling at
The cord
Reaching out
To her

VITALITY

Through the mist
Through the fog
Through the clouds
Hoping that
One day
She'll finally
Reach back.

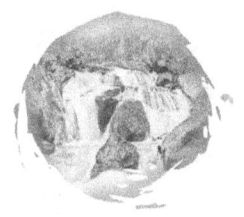

UNFINISHED HEARTS

The broken-hearted
Boys
And the broken-hearted
Girls
Who felt too
Deeply
Moved on
From this
Broken
Part of the world
Leaving behind
Unfinished
Hearts.

VITALITY

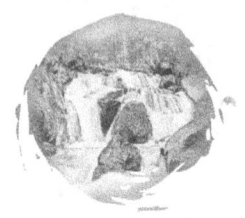

SEQUENCE

All this life
Really is
Is a
Sequence
Random
Non-uniform
Continuous

I've
Never
Had
The ability
To
Retain
Much
Except
For
The little
Things

Like you
Talking about
Getting your mother
That jeep she likes
So much
With your first
Paycheck
Or insisting
On stopping
At every small
Shop on the way
For chocolate ice cream
Or preferring
The walk back
Home
Over the drive;

I retain
Those small
Elements
In bottles –
And the bottle caps
Are just the trail
With no clear
Beginning

And they end
Right there
Just across

VITALITY

The small
River

The one
You also mentioned
You like
So much.

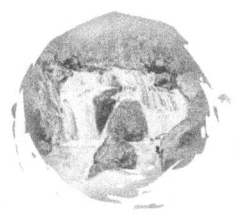

How long

How long
Before
Our defenses
Fall
How long
Before
Our walls
Crumble down
How long
Before
The surfacing fables
Dissolve
How long
Before
We learn
To love
Again?

VITALITY

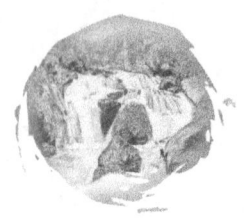

WE ARE

We are
A dying
Nation
Left in
The wake
Of burning
Cinders
To soak up
The smoke
And bask
In
The flames.

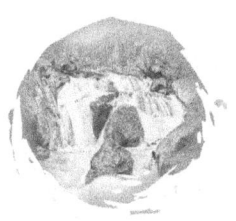

No Matter

No matter
What they say
About us
Whether they say
We were good
Or incompatible
Or a mistake
Or a bad phase

I will remember
You
I will remember
Us
Like I remember
The sweet taste
Of bourbon
By the fireplace

I will remember

VITALITY

Your being
Close to mine
How every one
Of your breaths
Spread warmth
In the channels
Of my body

I will remember
You and me
Together
When time froze
And when it sped by

I will remember us
Together

And darling,
We were
Golden.

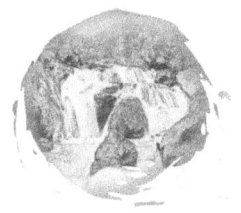

FREIGHT TRAIN

Swallowing
Heartache
After
Heartache
I wait
For the day
I will meet you
On an unknown
Freight train
Passing through
Some cities
Heading
Someplace

And I will sit
Next to
Your backpack
Containing
A roughed up

Vitality

Map
Of the
World
That you
Scratch off
Bit by bit
At
Each
New
City

And I will
Be carrying
Only
This notebook
And photograph
Our little talks
The exchanges
We held in our
Eyes
For so long
Before pouring
Them
Onto
Each
Other
I will
Write down
The brown coffee

Served with sockets
Of white sugar
The mahogany
Bench we sit on
I will scribble
Pieces of
The view
The magnificent
Landscape
That takes over
And transposes
The mind
From city smog
To green pastures

And you will
Look at me again
With that unique
Look of yours;
That naïve
Almost innocent
Contemplative
Sweet
Stare
That you
Have effortlessly
Made yours
And offered it
To the world

VITALITY

As a trademark
Just as many
Film directors
Made signatures
Out of specific
Shots

And you will
Say,
'Don't
Write
About
Me
Anymore'
Darling,
Anything
Is worth
Writing
About

And as you fold
The pages
I hand you
And think of me
As just another
Stranger
You met
On the train
I will have moved

On
To
The
Next one
Forgetting
The drinks
The bats that perch down
My ceiling
During stormy nights
The city folks
The white strips
On the sidelines
The loneliness
The anger

I will have
Moved on
To
The next page
And scratched it off
As we pass through
Another city
Marking yet again
What my heart
Has repetitively
Failed to declare:
A glimmer
Of hope
Re-instated

VITALITY

A new breath
Filling my lungs
And another
Promise
Of a renewed
Meeting
With
You
Somewhere
On
A
Freight train.

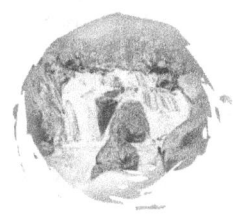

OBSERVATION

There is
Something
You and
I
Both
Don't know

It's that
This same
World
Capable
Of such
Fluctuating
Madness
Is also
Capable
Of resounding
Bits
Of magic:

VITALITY

It sometimes
Leads us
To paths
We were
Unaware of

Or rarely
Conjures
Moments
Worth
Remembering

Even
Occasionally
Writing about

Like arriving
In front of a house
We know
After a long drive
In the middle of the
Night

Or
Meeting
A familiar
Face
At
The
Movies

Or
Bringing back
A silly
Memory
At a birthday
Party;

These
Moments

These precious
Little cutouts
Of our lives

Make writing
People in
More bearable
More pleasant
More interesting

They make it easier
To forget
The same world
That is dictated
By two-story suicide
Dives
Through glass windows
And highway accidents
And ghetto

VITALITY

Neighborhood
Turbulence

They make us forget
About hardships
And heartbreaks
Even for
A short while

And focus instead
On the moments
That matter:

The ephemeral
Little looks
The flirty
Conversations
The brief touches
The reclusive whispers
That lead to wild drives
With the radio music on

The good
Little moments
We often
Forget about
And swallow whole

The moments
We deduct

From our speeches
And our writing

The moments
That aren't
So
Little

The moments
That define
The lines
That make us

These moments
Beat off
Any symphony
Any piece of prose
Any canvas
Exploding
With vibrant colors

They
Make us
Human.

VITALITY

WHEN

Most of them
Wanted to become
Writers
Of the modern era
And write
Clever lines
On subway walls

But being
A writer
Wasn't
Something
You became
It was
A disease
You were
Born with
That turned you
Beastly

In the darkest hours
Of the night
And made you
Reject
Society
And sometimes
Even
Humanity
Entirely –

But they all
Chose
To neglect
Those
Details
For the
Glory
And the
Fame;

And so
Here they are
Out
In the world
Going about
Their
Lives
While I sit
Here

Vitality

> And
> Write
> My
> Lines.

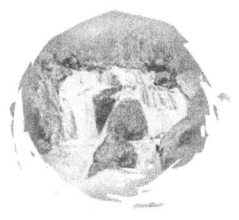

BASIC NEED

I still
Couldn't
Understand
The basic
Need
Of people
Belonging
To
Each
Other

It seemed
Like
A selective
Formula
Designed
For
A specific
Group

Vitality

Of the
Population

But
Having
So many
Of them
Adhere
To
It
Makes me
Wonder
How long
I can keep
Hiding
Behind
The shades
Of
My
Words.

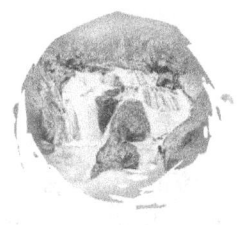

INSANITY

Living
Vicariously
Through other
People
Was insanity
And living
Through
The readings
Of others
(No
Matter
How
Prophetic)
Was also
Insanity.
Some people
Were driven
To madness
Without

VITALITY

Knowing
How
Or
Why
While others
Were pulling the ropes
While holding the blade
Between their
Teeth.

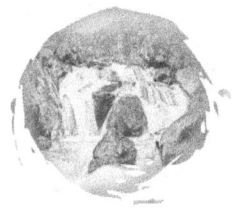

OVERSHOOT

A man's
Heart
Contains
All the
Love
For
His
Woman
And
Sometimes
A little bit
Of
Whiskey
Too.

VITALITY

LITTLE GIRL WITH DARK EYES

There is
A little girl
With dark eyes
I know
Who used to say
Every day
Is a good
Day.

Even when
The traffic jam
Is clogging
The city
On rainy days
Or you come back
Late to your apartment
And are constantly
Interrupted

By power cuts
Or you try
To turn on the heater
On cold winter nights
And it won't work
The little girl
With dark eyes
Would say
Every day
Is a good
Day.

I knew
A lot of women
And most of them
Weren't very good
But this girl
Belonged
To the good ones.

VITALITY

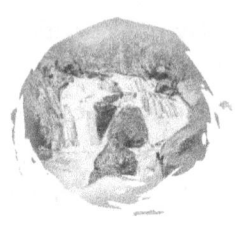

SOME DREAM

And in
Your wildest
Dreams
You would like
To hold her
In your arms
Like some kind of
Beautiful Madonna
Stare into
Her caring eyes
And hear her
Whisper
She would like
To see you
Again

Her lips,
So fragile

And you,
Thinking back:

> I'll
> Hold
> You
> To
> That.

VITALITY

In this city

But being
In the same city
Made little
To no
Difference
At all;
Our lips
Held the words
But our mouths
Wouldn't utter
Them.

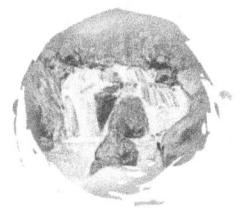

CRAWL

Crawling closer
To the edge
Every day
Amid portraits
Of faces
I used to know:
Some of them
Family members
Others friends
Others past lovers

I crawl past ex-girlfriends
Women I used to know
And hold hands with
And offer flowers
Or nice bottles of wine
I crawl past acquaintances
Rivals
Enemies

VITALITY

People who diminished me
People who tried to bury me
People who held up a gun
And stuck it against my forehead

I crawl past the walls
The pictures
The memories
The eerie distant voices
Of broken silences
In small rooms
Where small men discussed
Small ideas
Surrounded by their small women
Past laboratories and college halls
Where every human being was an experiment
Past public libraries
Filled with troublemakers
Troubled souls
Searching for salvation

I crawl under the rug
It is raining outside
It feels good to be
Under the rug
Under the world
Under the weight
And to feel light
Ever so light

Almost invisible and weightless
Like a feather
Falling to the floor
Smacked away by the kicks
Of trespassing people
Rushing for more
Always rushing for more
Of life
More of this
More of existence
While others crawl behind

I crawl under the rug
Forgetting the faces
Forgetting the kicks
Forgetting the people
Even if just
For a minute.

VITALITY

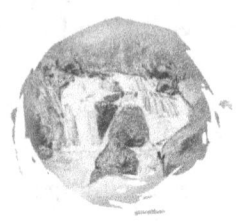

FALLOUT

Another vision
Of her:
This time
At the movies
With her girl friend
Carrying her large
Butter popcorn
Walking around
In her tanned
Sunburnt
Skin tone;

Even a
Miracle
Can't save
Me
Now.

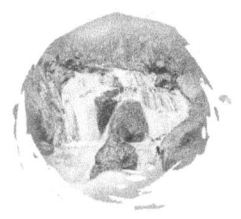

KILLING SOFTLY

I watched a man standing
On the outside window
Of a building
'That's one good way
To get killed off,'
I thought
Before looking down
At the page
In front of me:
And here
Is
Another.

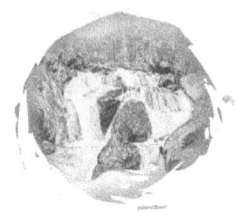

BLAME

We are blamed
For not entertaining
Social ideologies
We are blamed
For not speaking up
We are blamed
For rebelling
We are blamed
For loving
We are blamed
For carrying the roses of death
And marching up and down
Hell's avenue.

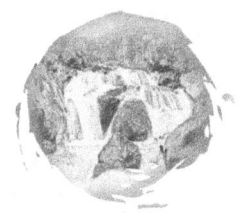

DESTINED

The cat
Is up in
My face
It licks
My nose;
Another
Woman
Has
Left.
The cat
Is up
In my
Face
It licks
My nose;
I am
Destined
To
Endure

Vitality

This life
Alone.

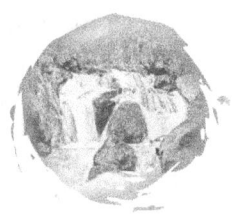

NO MORE LINES

Don't read these lines;
Don't read these lines
Or any other line
I write.
They say the human brain
Is different for men
And women:
Women
Are better
At processing
Things
Assessing
Situations
While men
Are faster
In falling in love.
Well
It has taken me a lifetime –
Not in years –

VITALITY

But it has taken me a lifetime
In words,
Pages,
Songs maybe
To fall in love
With her.
I have been through
The sickness
Of longing for
A good woman;
I have been through the chants
And reprieve
And threats
And warnings
Of chasing her.
But I've come back now
I've returned from the dark
Back to the page
Where it all began.
The bruises on my shoulders
Are barely showing
The concussion
Is barely there
But I am here to write
The lines that will prevail.
These won't be the lines
That will erase it all;
These won't be the lines

That erase the moment
When we split a cold dessert
Late at night
And she instinctively placed her head
On my right shoulder;
These won't be the lines
That erase the state
Of jealousy and fury
She put me through
When she said another man
Had eyes for her.
No,
These won't be extraordinary
Lines.
They will be the lines
That will stay
For the record books
The lines in the sand
The ocean water can't wash off
Or wipe away
They will be the lines
That plummet the dark
They will be the long-standing
Figure of survival.

Most importantly
They will be the lines
She will not read
The lines

VITALITY

I will
Forever
Keep.

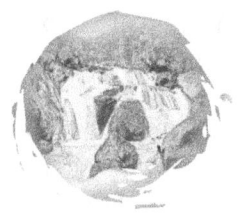

Final letter

There is a space
Between you
And me
The space
Between silence
And white noise
Water drops from
The shower tap
Running down
The body

There is a space
Between you
And me
An incurable
Disease
That spreads
Throughout the body

And fills the pores
And open wounds

There is a space
Between you
And me
The holes of
The small radio
Playing 90s tunes
In the dark

A brave young man
Whose shattered heart
Can be heard
From the top of the street

A fair woman
Who has dealt with
Loss after loss
Broken heart
After broken heart
Who never gives in
Anymore
Who never opens up
But instead chooses
To put up more frontiers
To protect her heart
Irreversibly
She thinks about
All the men

That have come and gone
All the men
Who promised to stay
And love faithfully
And cherish
But have disappeared
Like the last summer wind

She remembers all the men
She remembers them all
Except for the brave boy
Who appeared a lifetime ago
But couldn't make the promise
To stay.
The boy
Promised instead
To travel with her thoughts
Wherever they went
And wait
Wait for the ruins
To pick themselves up
And re-structure as
Golden pillars
Wait for the sieges
Of the world
To end in harmony
And music
Wait for the glory days
Of the artists and savants

VITALITY

To be restored.
He promised her to wait
He promised her to wait
But in return
She had to learn
To open up her heart
And they would both
Acknowledge and keep
Their end
Of the bargain
In such a way that
The morning she would awake
From her bed
And decide to unlock
Her heart
And throw away the keys
Into the vast sparkling sea
She would infallibly know
He would be the one
Waiting for her.

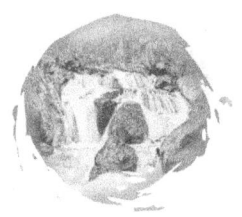

INFINITE

Picture this moment:
A thousand blinding
Suns
Hanging above
Your head
While you sit
In a shack
With the most
Beautiful girl
In the world.
Neither of you
Says a word
But her eyes
Alone
Tell a story
The most genuine
Writers
Have failed
To write.

LITTLE FEARS

I grow fearful
In the night;
I grow fearful
In the night
That branches out
Into the wide world
I grow fearful
In the night
That spreads
Like wild vultures spread
Their wings
Before a feast

We are afraid.

We are scared
Human beings
Scared of separation
Scared of distance

Scared of heights
Scared of change.
And those of us
Who raise their voices
Those of us
Who shout out through
The speakers of the world
Those of us
Who stand on altars
Pose in front of pillars
And address the world
From temples
Are no different
Than the rest;
They are no different
Than the passersby
That pull up at red lights
And are startled back to reality
By the honking of the vehicles
Behind them;
They are no different
From the youngsters
Living abroad
In small rooms
Sacrificing their health
And wellbeing
For the foreign experience
For the foreign life

VITALITY

They are no different
From the locals
Breathing the same air
The same polluted air
That governments and politicians
Are immune to
The same air
That constitutes smoke clouds
Above our heads:

We are afraid.

And to go back
To where I came from
Is an impossibility –
I am at an impasse
And while a detour
Seems unlikely
What lies ahead
Uncertainty
Mischievousness
Temptation
Solitude
Are most certainly
Far worse;
But the sacrifice
The weight we always attribute to it
The belief that it will make
Better men and better women

Out of us
Is always worth
The struggle

And now
Writing this
I question my motives
I question my beliefs
I question my honesty
And the honesty of my words
I question
My credibility.

To sit here
And watch from my foreign window
My foreign world —
A serene and magnificent
Place
Where dreams seem real
Touchable
And likely

I think back
Of the places
The street signs
The people
I have crossed
To get here:
Was the struggle
Worth the sacrifice?

VITALITY

It is a strange mix
Of feelings
But in times like these
I wish to say
That writing helps
But where the lines prove
Ineffective
There is always something else
Possibly residing in the heart
That keeps
A man
Going.

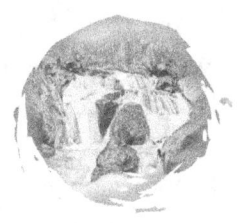

CREATION

I examine the digital
Clock beside me
It is 7:00 pm.
The girl next door
Is laughing with her boyfriend
While I am situated
On this floor
Trying to come up
With a few lines.
Whatever
Did inspire me
To take this road?
And while life is brimming downstairs
In the hallways
In the streets
In the sewers
I sit here
And try to relate it
All on paper.

VITALITY

And to deal
With this curse
This melancholy
Of existence
Is nothing new;
It is a sickness
That develops
That comes and goes
With every writer
At various stages
Where he is alive
And not alive
Where he is caught
Between life
And an impression
Of life.
As the hand steadily weaves
On sheets of paper
Sheets that get thicker
And thicker
Denser and denser
I wonder
For how long
I should keep drinking
From this cup.

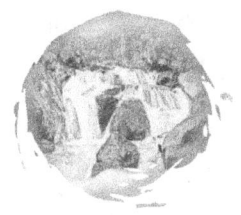

REMEMBER ME

Do remember me
By my words
Remember me
From the scribbles
On the walls
Remember me
From the screams coming
From the corridors
Remember me
From the glass shattering
On every apartment floor
Remember me
Through the bottle
You did not reach for
And touch
Or drink
Remember me
From the book you didn't read
Remember me

Vitality

By the words
You didn't say.

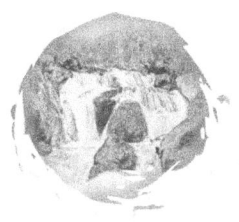

PEACHES FOR MY ROSES

**

She walked barefoot
On the sand
Carrying a book
I had written
Flipping the pages
Examining each line
Dissecting every poem

**

Each time
She came across
A poem about her
She would stop
Inhale deeply
And look at me
Timidly
Timidly

VITALITY

As if she was holding her breath
Steadfast

**

She would measure her words
Pause
Listen to the voice
Telling her to
Tread lightly
And I would anticipate
Her question
I would get ahead of
Her curiosity
Her unsuspecting soul
Eager to know
'Is this poem
About me?'
Yes, darling, it is.
Yes, it is.

**

Each time she came across
Another one
The same expression
Would pop up
On her face
As if she were reluctant
Or refusing
To accept

The answer
The unwavering truth
Coming out effortlessly on its own
Without me having to utter
A single word

**

And I would stand there
Admiring her
Admiring the way she held
That book
Timidly
Softly
Gently
While I was the triumphant fisherman
Who had just landed the biggest catch
I was the heroic sailor
Who had navigated the stormy seas
And made it back to shore

**

And to tell her
To tell her
I would've sent all the languages
Spiraling down to the depths of hell
Just to write
A perfect set of lines
That would come bursting through the middle
Of that book

VITALITY

And split it in half
So that she would find pieces
Of herself
In both

**

But she was ahead
Of me
She was always ahead
And had made it
To the last poem –
The longest of the bunch –
And intrigued
And curious
And playful
As always
She asked me about this one
And why it had lasted
To the end

**

The obvious answer –
My obvious answer
Was that I was made to believe
Most people
Didn't have the necessary courage
Or breath
Or patience
Or endurance

To make it to the end
Of a book
And most women
Mentioned in these lines
Were never able to hold their ground
Long enough
To last in it

**

And here she stared uncomfortably
Slightly parting her lips
Her eyes, unshifting
Unflinching
Still exuding that sweetness
She was known for

**

And at that moment
I didn't want to kiss her
Like any regular Everyman
At that moment
I only wanted to hold her hand
And walk with her
Take the long road
That leads to nowhere
Or maybe somewhere

**

Finally
Walking

Vitality

Towards me
Still holding the book
Close to her heart
Every bit of every poem
Written in it
Touching her soul
She asked me:
'Is this book
About me?'
A
Single
Question
To make me
Forget
The drunken nights
The demons flying
Overhead
The lonely places
I've wandered from
And to
Over the years
And the answer
Was even simpler
A brief
Brief gentle truth
That blew over her head
And caressed her silky hair:
This book is yours

And I love you
And I love you
And I love you.

**

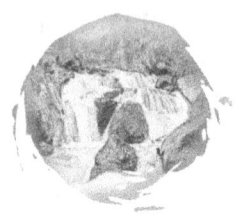

CAUGHT INSIDE A DREAM

And if I see you
In my dreams –
No, I don't want
To see you
In my dreams

Dreams are made
To be projections
Of the inhibitions of the heart
The ecstasy of the mind
The desires of the soul

And all these longings
Reflect in you

And when you are the barrier
Between what is real and what is not
That is where I'll be

Between life
And everything else

And waking up from
That near-perfect dream
Where we are alone together
In a small house during winter
Watching the snow fall on the windows
And accumulate on the ground
Makes everything else
Barely bearable
Barely livable
Barely acceptable

And so
To end this
Darling,
I would rather
Run into you
In a thousand lifetimes
Than in my dreams
But if I could
Cross you
Only once
On that line
Between life
And not life
Then maybe
That could be

VITALITY

A sign
Or a start
Of something
Real.

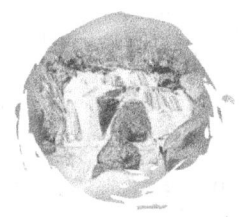

THE MOVE

It was during the sweetest sunset
On a barely memorable day
That I held her hand
And she said
Desperately,
'Forget me.
Forget me.
I will move away
For a long time
And you will forget me.
And if I come back
After a few years
You will have channeled
Those feelings
For another girl
And you will be madly in love
And happy.'

Vitality

'Darling,'
I said to her,
'You will move away
And I will be the local man
Jumping back and forth
Between the grocer
And the baker
Writing sonnets of old age
That may one day be imprinted on the walls
Of the underground
By some believer
Or non-believer
In god or the word
Or art or love.
I will be the local man
And when you show up
Again
I will look at you
The same way I look at you right now
And I will remember the touch of your hand
And the way the faint rays of the orange sun
Reflect on the side of your face
And I will have written many books
About you
Too many writings
For a single man to remember or cite
Aloud
And you will come back

And the sun will rise
And set again
Over the water
Just like now
And everything
That had ceased
To exist
Will live again.'

VITALITY

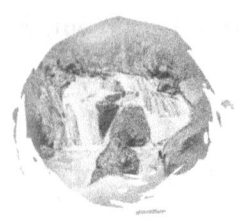

I SELDOM READ THE WRITERS

I seldom read the writers
I seldom read the writers
Who write about
Gorgeous women
And refer to them
As the most beautiful
They have ever seen.

That is the issue
With writers:
Even the great ones
Sometimes fall into
The glorification trap
Where they take anything
And make it grandiose
Beyond human measure.

I never believed that —
I never believed
Those words
And you shouldn't either
You should read the words
Of writers
With great caution
Like I do

And so now
I am here
To expose the profile
Of a woman
Who has never been the most beautiful
Or the most caring
Or the most charming;

I am here
To expose the profile
Of a woman
Who has always been
Soulful

And that alone
Is enough
For her
To transcend
Any form of descriptive
Text
Ever to be written.

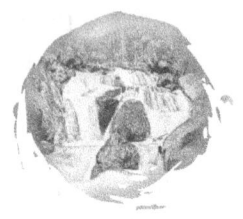

DECISIVE PEOPLE

Very few people
Were worth
Basing life decisions
On;
She was
One of them.

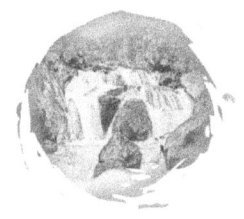

INFLUENCE

Odd
The way we heavily
Value a single
Human being
Above all others
Knowing they all belonged
To the same race
And could be traced back
To the same ancestry.

I have had my art
Trashed
By Arab friends
Foreigners
Strangers even
But a simple look from her
At one of my lines
Saying it touched her
Or spoke to her

VITALITY

Instantly rendered anything I wrote
Immortal

Conversely,
Having fans of my work
Constantly reach out to me
Whether by phone or mail
Or in person
To commend my writing
Was useless
As long as she reserved
No praise
For my words.

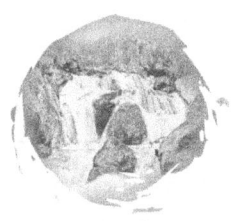

THE WRITING PROCESS

I will not lie
And say the writing process
Is easy —
You have to be prepared
For it to strike
Any time.
Whether it hits you
When you are out for a jog
Or at the office in front of your workstation
You will feel a pinching sensation
Urging you to get up
And pace the room
Pace the room
Until the thought has taken shape
And the structure is clearly laid out
In your mind.

VITALITY

This then
Is the lifecycle of a writer:
Constant interruptions
From the writing
Sneaking up on their everyday lives
Their love life
Their work life
And most writers will try to play it down
And convince you the writing is done
In a secluded remote room
Under the lamp light

But the truth is
It is a curse
It is a curse we have accepted
And willingly inflicted upon ourselves
The moment we have signed that demonic decree
Which states that we should write
We should write
We should write.

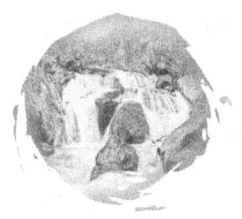

THE THINGS SHE LIKES

I realized
That I enjoyed
Listening to her
Speak about the things
She likes:
Ice cream
Peanuts
Long road trips along the beach coast
t.v. series
Books

But it was particularly
Books
I enjoyed listening to her
Talk about:
Works of fiction
Classics

VITALITY

Libraries she goes to
Her reading habits

I would dive into that world
With her
And believe me
When I tell you
Nothing
Or very few things
Have had a similar effect on me

Listening to her
Speaking about the books she enjoyed
The books she disliked
The books she couldn't wait to devour
Re-assured me of what I already knew:

She was
Like no other woman
I had ever met before
And unlike any woman
I would ever hope to meet:
Maybe it was the air
She spoke with
Or the choice of words
Which gave her a sense of
Naiveté
Perhaps?
No,
No

Hanna Abi Akl

It was innocence
Like no other
It was a flamboyant innocence
Akin to the one you observed
In the eyes of a child

It was bright innocence
Like the plumage of a peacock
It was innocence
Like the first painting of a prodigy
Laid out on a white canvas

And thinking of this
Right now
Brings me
To this conclusion:

I am glad
To have met her
I am glad
To know her
And I am glad
To be able
To listen to her
Recite the things
She likes.

VITALITY

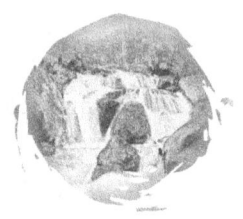

WONDERWALL

This mind is not made
To consume food ads
On the sides of pickup trucks
Or feed off pre-recorded televised news
Airing nightly on home stations
This mind is not made for
Football
Sports in general
Gossip
It is not made for dirty politics
Or religious discourse
This mind is a shallow cave
Where a river of darkness flows
This mind is an empty globe
A hard-rock shell
Ready to burst into pieces

I am not one to be concerned with
Trivialities

Or even necessities
I shun them in favor of what is truthful
And real;
And so
I set you up
Made you out of
Clay, brick, stone
But you are still breakable
Leaving cracks where the darkness penetrates
And infiltrates my mind

You are the boundary between me and the realm
Of reality
The platonic cave
The au-delà
I aspire to reach

But the cracks are real,
Darling,
And while they do not harm you
The slightest
They diminish me
They diminish my vision of the real
Of the pure

Still I lean on you
I lean on this vessel
Where the darkness slips
And infiltrates my veins
My bones

Vitality

My structure
And I fail to see through the faults
I fail to see through the flaws
Of this impressive structure
I built
This impressive gateway to you
From which the darkness escapes
I fail to see beyond the gaping holes
I fail to see through the cracks

The same cracks
Where a bit of light
Seeps in.

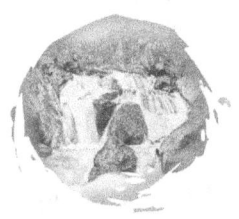

TO THIS LIFE

Perhaps,
I discovered,
The secret to all of this
Was not my burning desire to write –
It was
Writing
Finding
Me.

VITALITY

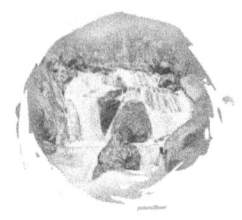

HIDDEN WORLD

I drink my coffee out on the terrace
The neighbor's two dogs
Are at it again
An old lady pushes her granddaughter
In a cart
This is my world;
This is the world I see

I think about you
I think about you
Showing me hidden parts of the world
Another world I am yet to explore
Through your accent
Your looks
The way you behave around me
And around other people

There is a hidden world
That is only made accessible
Through you

A world I see glimpses of
In drunken folly
Or dumbfounded sobriety

A world I feel strangely connected to
A permanent road I seek
A place I wish to inhabit
Forever.

VITALITY

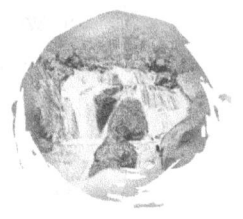

LETTER ONE

I sit here unable to write

Love,
I sit here and languish
In the pile of my successive defeats;
I am dancing between the lines
Thinking about your name
That rich
Rich heavy name
That almost-English name
Which reminds me of the gloomy city
But also of spring.

Love,
There is a spring inside me
A spring that you have violated
But if you ask me how I'm doing
Or how I've been for the past time
I will say good or bad

Or average
Whichever you prefer.

Love,
I am trying to convey the inexplicable
I am trying to write the words between my lips
Hanging at the edges of my mouth
The words that spread from me to you
That are covered by the breadth of your mouth
On a happy day

Love,
They say the sleepless man is the victim of life
But in this era
The loveless never get a chance
They are doomed to walk the stairs of the abyss
Like fading ghosts
Waning in cold sunlight

But they do not know what I know

They think of love as the twisted knife
While it can be a woman singing
While whipping her hair

They think of love as damnation
While it can be holding a maiden's hand
Come sunset

VITALITY

> They think of love as madness
> While it can be you
> Simply existing.

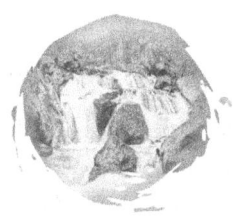

VEDETTE

She taps her feet lightly
To the tune of my guitar;
I have seen her at parties
Carrying her drink and mingling around
With strange foreign people I don't know
And do not wish to know
While I stand in my corner
Looking through an open window

The people are drunk;
The people here are drunk
In these late night parties
That drag on to the early morning
Awakened by the first sunrise
The sun rays creeping through my window
Sliding under my sheets
And pouring over my face
I think of the nights I spent alone
Alone in a room

VITALITY

Alone on the plane in some strange country
On a bizarre continent I had never seen before

I think of crossing her
In a random street
While she walks on a trail of stars
I think of crossing her
In front of her old badly-constructed house
Trampled and cramped in a tight neighborhood
That knows no light of day
No mercy during cold war-ridden nights
And no daylights in between

The places I go to –
In my mind at least –
Are not places I have visited before
They are the places she has traveled to
The places she plans on seeing
On star-ridden nights
Where a meteor shower can be spotted from a singular spot
On a camp site or a mountain top

She is lighting up parties
With her youth and beauty
In small apartments
While men around her crack open bottles
And I have never been good with parties
I have never been good with people

But on forgetful winter nights
When she is covered up to her nose
In her sheets
I am not the relentless poet
That draws on street walls
Or banishes the demons of the mad;
I am not the writer
Who will save the human race
From terrible and formidable injustice;
I am not the hero
That will be remembered in the books
Or receive prestigious medals for his achievements;

No,
On long forgetful winter nights
That stretch along the snowy avenue
When she is covered up to her nose
In the sheets
Beaten down by the cold
I am her man.

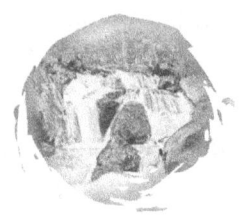

SAME ODE

I came back to the sofa –
The dirty colorless sofa

I have sat on that sofa nearly a million times
But this time was different:
This time I was disconnected from
every other being
In the universe

I was alone.

She sat next to me
And I started playing with her black hair
Sniffing it
Smelling every follicle on her scalp
And she placed her head on my chest
And let it sink there
Just sink
As if she were dipping it in a pool…

We talked
We drank
And the night wore on
The sofa
And the air
And the walls turned pale
And she spoke about leaving again
This time for good
She spoke about the great places
Europe
France
Making stops at extraordinary sites
Hopping from one train
To the next
And I hopped along with her
In my mind
I hopped on every stop
Of the way
But still I couldn't
Catch up to her

She spoke about her academic track
About submitting her research work
And I poured more wine
And lent my ear to the universe…

All I could do
Was whisper her name in the dark
Still now

VITALITY

I recall and retrace every step of that conversation
I re-enact the dialogues in my mind
I re-visit the sites she spoke of
The countries she cited
And still I am unable
To write down her name

Forcefully
I write forcefully tonight
Out of obligation and without any will
But these lines while forced must come out of me
Like a forced belch
Or a scribbled drawing

Tonight I see no end
No end to this country
No end to this madness
Just people chasing after their shadows
Interspersed in the corners of the globe

Little whores crawling around naked men
Seeking some form of validation
Tired men submitting to the hard jobs
To gain some assertion
People chasing after planes
And new lives perhaps

And she was no different –
She became no different

But holding her was still eternity
On that pale dusty sofa

Holding her – no matter
How briefly –
Was still eternity
And to tell her what I am about to write
Next
To tell her that
Knowing it wouldn't change a thing
Knowing she wouldn't believe it
To tell her that
In spite of my problems
And in spite of hers
Being with her
Solved most of it
No,
Being
With
Her
Solved
All of it.

WITHOUT KNOWING

Walking toward our meeting place
After a long day
Surviving the heat
Losing my money
Forfeiting the job

Walking toward our meeting place
With a stained white shirt
My shoes with holes in them
Tasting the concrete

And the thoughts arrive in streams
The things we push away
And try to hold off from our brains
For as much as we can
For as long as we can:

Tee, I love you
I hope I will make it tonight

I hope my car will start tomorrow
I hope I will find another job

I arrive to the place like an old-fashioned poet
Carrying nothing but his overcoat
And a stash of poems under his pits
Except there are no poems
The lines are jumbled in my mind
And they are not stashed
Stacked
Folded
Plied
They are jumbled in my mind

I hope to look into your eyes
And forget the day
Forget the week
Forget the upcoming tomorrows
The hustle
The struggle
The job
And the poems I haven't written

I hope you will order your favorite thing
And speak of the things you marvel at
And the things you find hard to understand
There she is now;
Waiting for me at the door
Her eyes
Keeping away the vigilantes

VITALITY

>The drunks
>The losers
>The men that have been zeroed out and
>Mutilated
>By women

>It was easy to become a drunk
>It was easier still to become
>A poet
>In a city like this
>In a time like this
>But it was hard
>To become a lover

>And tonight I still loved her
>And I was glad she didn't know
>The same way she wanted to tell me things
>Without my knowing

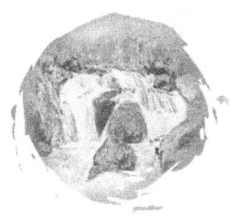

I AM THE CREATOR

I am the creator
You are the creation
The never-ending stone sculpture
The double-aged bottle

I am the creator
And you are the myth
That becomes more real
The more I try to understand it

You are the roots
Deeply rooted in my mind
The waves that cannot be silenced
By the storm

I am the creator
You are the creation
And I'd like to know
What you think
Of me.

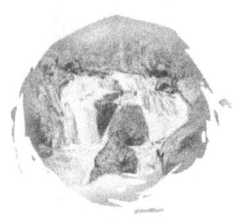

YOU CAN HAVE YOUR MEN

You can have your European men
In business suits
And leather briefcases
You can have your expensive trips
To fancy capitals

Just give me one night with you

To show you the underworld
The gritty streets
One night to show you
The alchemy that begins
With the breath of the poet
And ends on the page
The transformation that starts
With the touch of your hair lock
And ends in your heart

You can have your men
You can have your world tours
Just give me a single night
    With you.

VITALITY

OPEN YOUR HEART

You could see it
In the eyes of the old
The young
The handicapped
The ill
The healthy:

Their hearts
Were crippled

Crippled and old
Crippled and rotting
Crippled and closed.

Nobody stepped up
When it mattered
Nobody stepped down
For anybody
When it mattered –

Closed hearts
Were the real disease
Nobody could fight
Or find a cure for.

People getting separated
At airports
Because of a little distance

People allowing themselves
To drag on
Without each other
Instead of holding on
To what's real

People who fanned
The dying embers
Of the night
While refusing to soak
In the flame.

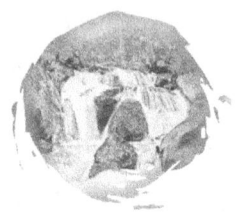

TRAVELERS

And she looked at me
Like a believer –
She looked at me
Like a preacher
Infused with the power of god

And she spoke about
Traveling
About the world
About the cultures
And the people
She spoke about expanding horizons
In a shrinking world
She spoke about developing my writing
About creating new experiences
About becoming a forgotten tourist
In some lost city
For a day

And I sat there
Half-looking at her
Half-looking at her green dress
That glimmered in the midday sun
Listening to dialogues about traveling
Only she was the one going away
To new beginnings;
She was the one
Reaching out for greater horizons
Taking deeper breaths into this small world
And I was still here.

Someday
They will write about the existential poet
Who made it in a small world
Not knowing the odes and sonnets and verses
He was made famous for
Were all written
For the traveling girl.

VITALITY

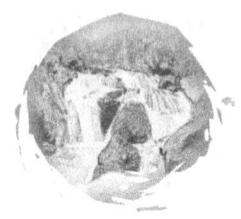

Bad days

Sure, I've got
My bad days
But even those
Manage to squeeze out
A few good words
Out of me

And at the end
Of it all
That's all
That really
Matters.

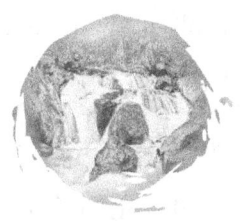

MY BEING

My being
Filtered into these sewers
Filtered into their homes
Filtered into these walls
Filtered into their minds

My being
Accompanying each lonely child
Each poor man
On a journey to redemption

My being
Filtered into the minds
Of 40-year-old bachelors
Into the skirts
Of red-headed prostitutes
Filtered into the alcoholic drinks
That sparkle with colors and madness

VITALITY

This place is a minefield
And the ropes are tightened at the perimeter
We enter into madness not knowing what to expect
And unknowingly stay there fearing

What's outside might be even worse
This place is a minefield
That my mind slithers through
It filters into its soil
All the way down to the roots
It touches the tips
And slowly surges back again

My being
Is in every sip you take
Each night you choose to be alone
Eclipsed from the world and its shadows
Hiding from the bright light
Like the convicts who still probe empty alleys
Hoping to find a safe place

My being
Is in every empty gaze you perceive
In every love you give away
That is not yours.

Hanna Abi Akl

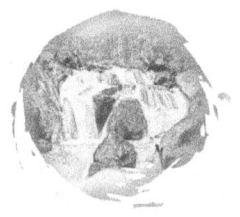

I DONT MISS ANYTHING

I don't miss the paper
Or the thick city smoke
I don't miss the little houses with red roofs
Or the traffic jams downtown
I don't miss the words
Or the music
I don't miss the bars
The drink
The smell of perfume on beautiful women

I don't miss the job
Or the paycheck
Or the buses
Or the cars

I don't miss the airport
Or the bookstores

VITALITY

Or the famous lines
Written by men far more famous than me

I don't miss the neighborhood
Or the streets
But sometimes –
Sometimes in my little apartment
I miss her
I miss her with the cup full
I miss her with the cup half-empty
I miss her with the cup fully
Drained.

And the previous whispers
The previous whispers she had done her best
To shut out
The previous whispers telling me I couldn't
make it
Have suddenly
Resurfaced.

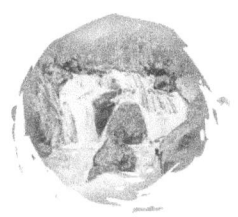

Joy

After a while
You understood there was little
Joy left in the world

And now
Right here
Sitting with her
Gazing from the acropolis
Looking down at the slumbering city
As the morning dew slowly washes away
Under the noon sun
I knew the only joy left
For me
Was with her

VITALITY

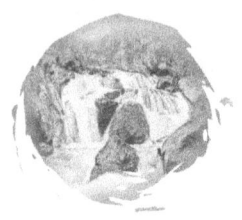

I WALKED FROM DOOR TO DOOR

As I walked
From door to door
With my book under my arm
Trying to find a decent buyer
I realized most of them
Were just looking for a way
To stay alive…

And I could hear the coffee pots brewing
In angry morning kitchens
The prayers in the bathroom stalls
The screaming graffiti on the public walls
The little infant cries marring hospital halls…

They were everywhere:
Mad
Loose

People of the streets
Aching for a way out

And as I filled the pages
So did their screams
Fill my head
And I walked with a heavy heart
The book trailing behind me
In empty streets
Empty neighborhoods
To the sound of melancholy birds
Chirping away at another sunset
That would lay waste to the day
And all its bearings

And so came another night
Filled with sorrow
Filled with music
Filled with broken hearts
Fears
And broken dreams
Crushed under metal palettes
And reinforced steel
Container trucks parked in front of art studios
While beer bottles chimed at the other end of
the street

I walked from door
To door
With my book

Vitality

Under my arm
Trying to find
A decent
Buyer
While most of them
Were still looking
For a way
Out.

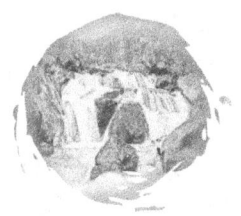

STILL WRITING AT 80

One day
I will wake up
Old and wrinkly
And look around me
To see everything
Is still fresh
And ripe;
The imported wine bottles
The ashtrays in the sitting room
Even the paint
On the kitchen walls
Only my soul will have been enslaved
By time
Then
And it will have done its time

VITALITY

When the brain starts to decay
There isn't much you can do
Or hope for

But if I'm still writing at 80
If I'm still in harmony
With the words
Then I'd likely look back
On my life
And call it a success.

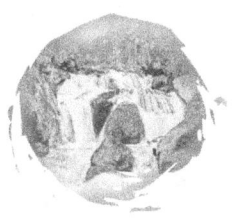

THE OPEN ROAD

Good music
A car
A good woman
And the open road

That was all
A man
Really needed.

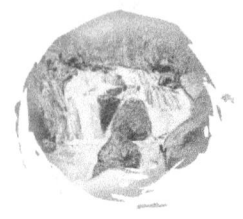

IF THEY ASK ME FOR THE TRUTH

If they ever ask me
For the simple truth
I will tell them
It is not religious
Social
Or political;
It is
Mathematical:

Between me
And her
No distance
Was great enough

Only I knew it
And she didn't
Yet.

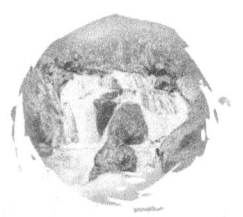

I BEAT A MAN AT THE POOL TABLE

I beat a man at the pool table
And he sneered and jeered at me

I beat a man at the pool table
And the band was still playing
Late 80s songs

I beat a man at the pool table
And the lead singer –
A young gypsy girl in tight overalls –
Was giving me the eyes

I beat a man at the pool table
And glared at him
And drank his beer

I beat a man at the pool table
And thought about closing down the bar

VITALITY

I beat a man at the pool table
And shoved another on the way out
Just because he couldn't quote Hemingway

I beat a man at the pool table
And returned to the desk
Returned to the paper

Returned to the words
Returned to the calming influence
Of the woman that urged me to write
Always standing behind my thoughts
Like a shadow or a veil
Protecting me

Protecting me from my world
Relieving me from all my humane duties

Pushing me through the mud
Pushing me through the sand dunes
Pushing me through the streams
Pushing me through the vines and tombs

Pushing me to write:
'Write 100 pages'
She said
And I contested her
'Write 98 pages'
She said
And I contested her

And she kept going down
Narrowing the number of pages:

'Write 1 page'
She said.

Well honey
This
Is
The
One.

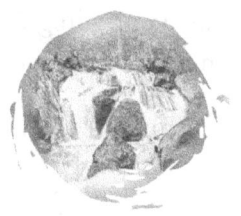

HER

I was drawn back to the late night conversations
With her
Coming home late from the office
Reeking of alcohol
My stale mouth tasting the excess coffee
And her
Calling me up to ask about
The mundanities of my day
Bypassing the atrocities I'd undergone
And striking right through to my heart

And in all honesty I would tell her
It was a good day
It was a good day
And forgetting the foul words
The foul people that had latched on to me
And crawled inside my skin
I would slide in my long chair and listen to her
Listen to her talk about her day

Imagine her moving her lips and swinging her hair
Like a jolly little girl

It was a good day
It was a good day
And the irony of it
Is that you can never really tell
Before it's truly over

And having her
Close the day
Was like drinking a cold beer
Under the hot summer sun:
Refreshing
Reinvigorating
Rejuvenating

And finally
Hearing her say good night
Hearing her words only
In the quiet of the night
Was the second chance I needed
To face a new tomorrow.

VITALITY

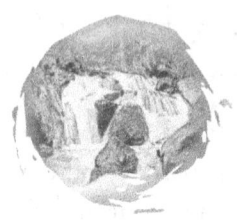

POWER CUT

Another power cut
The walls are empty
The factories are shut
Their desks overflowing with paper

The plant is open

The elevators cringe
On their way down to the bottom floor

There is a current
Entering through the bathroom window

My desk
Illuminated
By the faint lamp
Gives away the scribbles and carvings of my soul

The portrait of a great writer
Urges me to drink
And put on

Some classical music
But I bask in silence
Even the great writers
Are prone to bad judgements

I bask in silence
There is a current
Entering through the bathroom window

And I bask in silence

The desk suddenly clears itself
Of all the clatter
The paper the scribbles the carvings
The lights the noise
The people
The music the drink
The portrait of the great writer

Another power cut
And I bask
In silence.

VITALITY

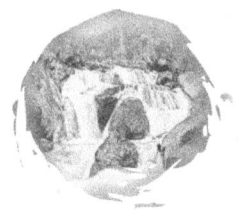

THE LAST TIME

The last time I saw her
Was when we sat together on the sidewalk
Facing an old fixed-up church
Staring at the scratch marks on the wall

She held the universe in her eyes
And I held her in mine

Back then
The lines only came easy
When I was with or around her

Now I write
Ground-shattering words
That break the earth in half
And if I see her again
If the next time I see her is the last time
I am sure
She will show up with that same smile
Those wandering eyes

That free-flowing hair
And the little giggles in between
I am sure
I will greet her
Like I have the first time:
With the same intrigue
We greet strangers
Who unwillingly captivate our hearts

And the weakness that never dies
The fear that stems from
The last time
The last goodbye
The last rotation of the earth
Will only harden and grow
Until the next time
The next giggle
The next few lines
I write
About her.

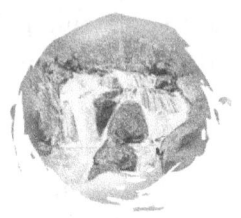

VISIONS

I have visions
Of myself
Coming home
Late from work
And her
Alone
In my apartment
Waiting for me

Her flower dress
Covering her legs
All the way down
Touching the ground

Her silky hair
Shining
In the moonlight

If ever there was
A perfect dream

To save us from this world
Then this was
The closest thing
To it.

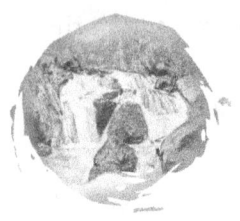

HOLY TRINITY

I have always believed
In the Holy Trinity

And before indulging
In any type
Of laborious work
I always recite the Holy Prayer:

I write for Truth,
I write for Justice,
And I write for Love.

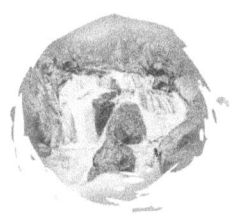

THE THREAD

I'm walking on the thread
The thread of no return
Hinged ever-so-slightly
Almost off-balance
Out
Of
Focus
Between life
And no life…

There is no gravity here
No matter
No rules to govern
This free fall…

I'm walking on the thread
The thread of no return
Hinged ever-so-slightly
Between life

Vitality

And no
Life.

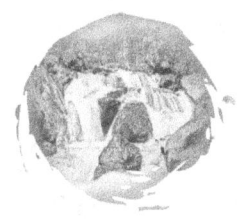

VITALITY

The three of us
Sat across each other
In the room
Each staring into the distance
The evaporating void

I was sitting on an old rusty couch
The springs popping out of its legs
And showing
The fabric bare
Destroyed by repetitive stain-cleaning
And Time
I held the bottle firmly in my right hand –
A warm bottle of whiskey that tasted like urine –
And rubbed my month-old beard with the other

The guy sitting across me was my best friend
And he was a clean guy
Until this moment

VITALITY

When I watched him light a cigar
And smoke it entirely
Effectively burning down
All the care in the world

The girl sitting with us had an ominous look
She bore the look of a prophet
Foreseeing the end of the world

All three of us were wrapped
In this thin layer of smoke
Bad alcohol
And bad luck

It was the rut
Alright;
The dirty skid
That went on endlessly
In the form of sinuous slopes

And with no end in mind we watched on
Waiting for the night to pass
And another day to crack through
Our windows…

Almost two-thirds into the bottle
The girl moved in next to me on the couch
And without warning grabbed my hand
And locked it in hers
She snatched away the bottle from me

And placed it gently on the rug
Beneath my feet…

It was one of those moments
You can't fully remember
No matter how hard you try –
The speed with which they happen
Overtakes you
But leaves you with some kind of impression
That things were perhaps steering toward a better ending
Or at least some kind of ending

The guy facing us was still sitting there
Observing the whole thing
And when he saw what the girl had done
To prevent me from walking over the edge
He dispatched the pack of cigars he hid
In his jacket pocket
A breast pocket I never knew existed

Seeing him rise again
From the ashes he worked so hard to create
And bury himself in
Made me swallow
For the first time
And the clot that was hanging there
In my chest
Blew into a thousand little pieces

Vitality

It made me see
There was perhaps
A better ending
To this
A better ending waiting
For all of us
Or at the very least
Some sort of
Ending.

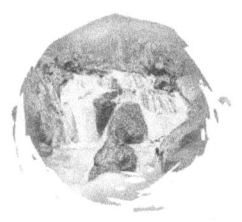

TO THE WOMEN IN THIS BOOK

I hope to someday
Fill your hearts
The same way
You filled
My lines.

VITALITY

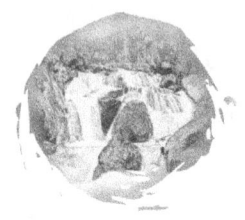

SKYLINE

Down,
Broken,
Beaten
And bruised
I leaned the half-empty
Bottle
Against the wall
And looked at the skyline.
The city was quiet –
No quieter than usual –
But there was minimal activity.
The horizon was clear:
In fact,
It was bright.
Yes, it was
Bright
For the first time.
I stared into the horizon
Piercing the dark clouds

And said:
'This
Is my skyline
Now'.
And I left
The half-empty bottle there,
Untouched.

VITALITY

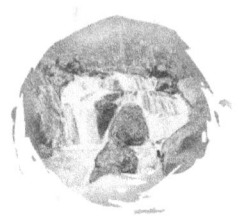

Playing for keeps

Always writing
The unnecessary lines
F i l l i n g t h e g a p s
Just to keep up with
The word…

Those who get up
After the sun
Find themselves trailing
And swallowed whole by the day

And those who rise
Before it
Have already disappeared
By nightfall

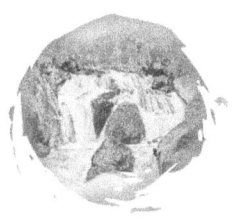

NO GOOD

What good was it
To be published
Or writing
Or even drinking
If it didn't get you any closer
To being alive?

VITALITY

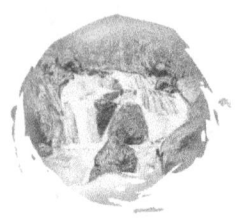

SOMETIMES

Sometimes
That's just the way
Words worked –

They aligned themselves
In perfect symmetry
Or perfect
Asymmetry
And exposed all the fears
Of the human race:

The things we whisper
To ourselves
While we lie awake
Late at night

The things we don't dare think of
And relegate to the farthest recesses
Of our minds

The things we do to each other
    But never
    Speak of.

VITALITY

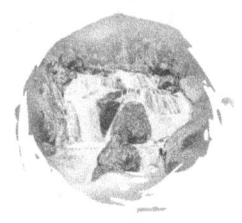

THE GLASS

There is nothing
Left
Between me
And the
Glass.
I've bottled
My whole goddamn
Life
Into it.
And now
I watch it
Slowly drink
From itself
And shrink
Away
Fading between the solid lines
Of the ice cubes

And the glass remains

And the glass
Remains.

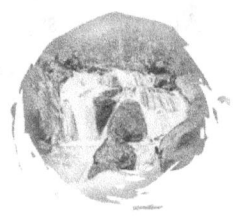

HALF

Half
The writers
Are good;
The other
Half
Aren't real.

Hanna Abi Akl

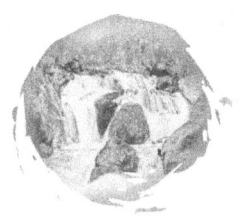

HEAVY WORLD

Priests accused
Of molesting children
Nuns raped
And murdered inside church walls
Rabbis tied to wooden chairs
Stripped and shaved and painted on
With the blood of the faithless
Mosques taken down
And replaced with state fairs

Sin is a virtue
Preaching is blasphemy
Mass and choir have become
Poor renditions for the ill-taught

God himself
Can no longer save them
From the devil

VITALITY

>It's a heavier world
>Now.

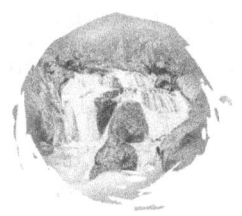

THE GOOD LINES

I'm drinking early tonight.
I'm staring at the page
Waiting for the good lines
But they rarely
If ever
Come.
The great poets
Will tell you
They sacrificed a lifetime
Searching for them
In vain
But I found them –
I find them
On rare occasions.
I find them
When she appears
In my thoughts
Like a thief in the night
When she gallops

VITALITY

Through the darkness
Surrounding my mind
The good lines
Come and go
As she pleases.
And the tragedy
The tragedy
In all of this
Is that they are bound
To her:
They come and go
As she pleases
They appear
And vanish
Along with her.
And my fear
My trembling fear
Is that they will never
Come again
If she ever leaves.
If she were
To disappear
Like this glass in my hand
Then the good lines
Will go away
As well
Up in smoke
Downsized into nothingness

Relegated to specks of dust
The roaches amuse themselves with.
Is she disappears
If she stops visiting the chambers of my mind
Then so too will the good lines.
And a man who loses his lines —
A man who is deprived the ability
To put down his words
Is a warrior without a shield
Naked and cold
His soul ripe and ready
For the taking.

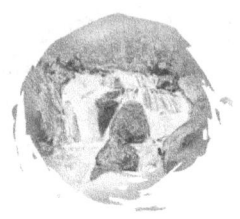

Where do the masses go

Where do the masses go
They head into the suburbs
They crawl inside the sewer pipes
They march under burning bridges

Where do the masses go
They walk on train tracks
They wander into the little markets

I watch them go
Like mad sheep trying to chase
A pack of wolves
They are headed for the stream
Unaware that they cannot swim through the currents

I watch them go out
Like the last matchstick
That lights into a spark
Its flame burning explosively

Cutting through the thin air
Lighting the candle
In a neighborhood home with no electricity

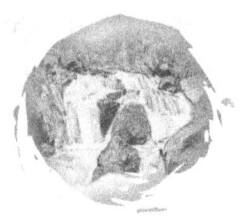

TODAY

The doorbell
Rang:
It is the man
With the water bill.

Tomorrow
I will wake up early
And go to work.

Today
I drank my usual pint
I thought about her
I paid my water bill
And I tried to write

I drank my usual pint
I paid my water bill
I thought about her
And now
I am trying to write.

Tomorrow
I will wake up early
And go to work

And I will think
About her.

There you go.

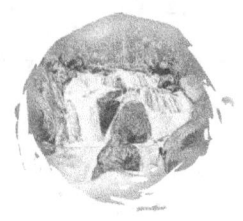

FALL BACK

I overload myself
Like a machine gun
Fill my arsenal with words
And unload them
On any wasteland
Before me.
But we all fall back
At some point:
Some of us
Fall back on something
And some of us
Fall back
On someone.
For me, dear,
It is the word –
I fall back
On the word
But my word
Isn't strong enough

And so
It falls back
On you.

VITALITY

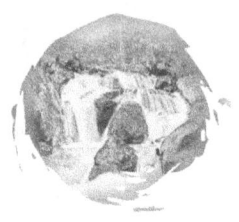

ONE MORNING

'Baby,'
I said,
'I have reason to believe
I'm great.'
She grabbed the bottle
From the counter next to me.
'And this?'
She said.
'Oh,
That's just something I think about
When I wake up'.
'And me?'
'You're the other thing
I think about.'
She smiled.
I looked at her rosy lips.
I believed
I could drown
In them.

Hanna Abi Akl

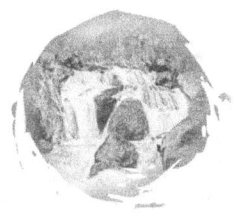

HANDS OF LOVE

Those who love and live
Often never tell the tale
And those who die
At the hands of love
Never live
To hear it.

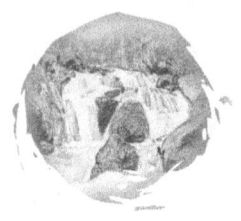

RUMINATING

Ruminating
Here alone
On my own
I drank
All there is
To drink.
Now,
There are things
I would like to share with you
Beyond the niceties
Of everyday conversation
But they risk driving you
Even farther away from me;
Already without you
I find myself lost
Lost in my own world
In my own home
At the bottom of my own glass
And to risk

Losing you entirely
Would be like
Throwing away
All the pieces of myself
Altogether.

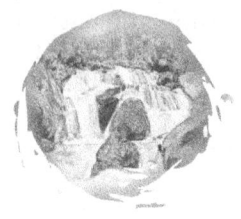

BURNING DESIRE

Those who create art
Are the mad ones,
The uncanny ones,
The unnatural ones,
The bastards, even
But today I am not one of them
Today I do not write to escape reality
Today I am the sea
Crashing against the shore
Crashing against the burning rocks
Engulfing them
To someday maybe leave
A few foot marks in the sand.

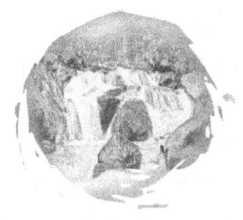

EMPIRE

Let me build an empire
That starts and ends at your feet
Let me build an empire
That runs down your hair
And touches your waist
Let me build an empire
That curbs down your back
And dissolves at your soles
Let me build an empire
That comes out of your throat
Let me build an empire
That surges from your eyes
Let me build an empire
With the complexion of your lips
Let me build an empire
With the fabric of your skin
Let me build an empire
From the mold of your hands
Let me build an empire

And frame it in your palms
Let me build an empire
That holds together with your voice
Let me build you an empire
With the seeded words you plant in me
Let me build you an empire
With every breath you latch at my face
Let me build you an empire
With the only tune I know
Let me build you an empire
And water it with alcohol
Let me build you an empire
With the collected works of my soul
Let me build you an empire
And armor the gates
And lock the door
And wrap it with a veil of dust
That turns into a sandstorm
Let me build an empire
And conceal myself in it
With you
So that maybe
We may hear the tiny flapping
Of thin paper
Against the window pane
On a summer morning
Again.

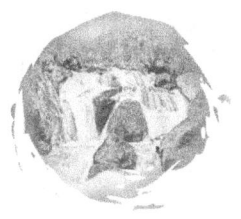

THERE IS A LIGHT INSIDE YOU

My dear,
There is a light inside you
That shines on this corner of the street
There is a light inside you
That turns on the street lamps
At night
My dear,
There is a European light
A foreign allure in you
That brings back the sweet scent of the land
There is something about you
That makes a man want to belong
More than ever;
That makes a man want to root himself here
In his home
Amid the small lights
And the stray cats

VITALITY

And the rabid dogs
And the crazy neighbors
And the dark alleys
My dear,
There is a light in you
That never stops shining
A light that flickers every time you speak
A light that drops on my world
I see it piercing through the cracks of my ceiling
I see it washing away my dirty floors
I see it climbing onto every piece of furniture
Swallowing every word I have ever laid down on fabric
My dear,
There is a light in this corner of the world
There is a small glint that flashes
Like a grain of sand on an Arabian night
And that light
Is you.

NEVER CALL YOURSELF A WRITER

Never call yourself
A writer –
Those who do
Fail to realize
That is the moment
They lose
Everything.

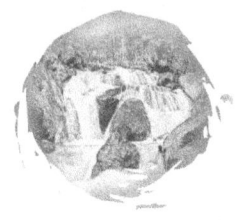

Different Universes

I have seen the eye of the raven
And it tells me stories
About different universes
Places where the poor
Governs the rich
And drunken men
Beat down their helpless sons
A place where You and I
Meet again for the first time
A place where you have traveled the world
And come back to the starting point
And I have met all the women
And drowned them in my torrent of waves
A place where I don't know your past
And you don't know my present
A place where I am certain of a future
That grounds me to you;

That is the place
I want to get to
That is the dream
I do not want to awaken
From.

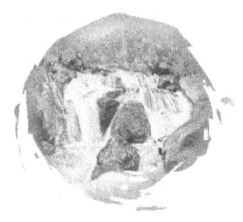

After me

There will come a time
When someone will come
And pick up my words
After me
And taint the lives
Of others
With them –
That is why
What was true then
Is true now:
We are creatures
Of the present –
We live for the rush
Of the heart;
The beating of every
Pulse;
And while I am unsure
There will be another sun
I will stick to

My single unifying
Point of truth:
Where you begin
So do my lines
And where my lines end
So do you
Close.

VITALITY

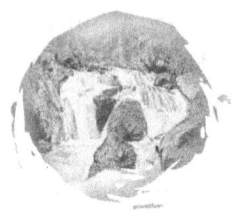

BANNERS

Banner men vouching for fake ideals
Carrying flags full of false hope
And false promises
You wondered how these people
Could rule the world by day
And sleep easy at night.

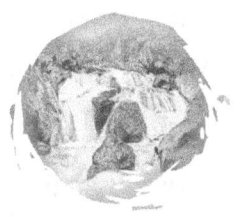

MY POETRY

There are simply things
You can't understand
Until you read them –
Things that are more personal
Than the most intimate touch
Or most discerning look

Today
I write to you again
To tell you that
We are more than our jobs
We are more than the distance
That confines us
We are more than the lives
That divide us

I write these lines
To narrow the gap
To shorten the distance

VITALITY

              Between us
            And to keep you
            Within my reach
            And
            Notwithstanding
The backlash of this troubled world
            I repeat myself
            Tirelessly
            Ceaselessly
            Endlessly:
            You
            Are
            My
            Poetry
You're the girl in my lines
You're the girl in my books
You're the girl in my heart.

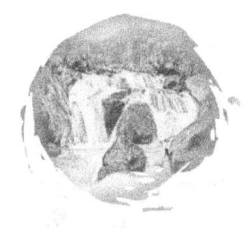

Run script

To hold onto something
So fragile
So delicate
Only to watch it break
After so long –
Or to watch it finally emerge
From the shadows
And step out
Into the light

To be able
To see your face
So clearly
After such a long time
Hiding in the dark
Finally

Vitality

Love
They say a man is lucky enough if he lives
To be a hundred
But to be able to see you in my own light
After chasing away the shadows in our realm
To be able to finally put down the bottle
After keeping it so close to me
For such a long time
To be able to echo your name
Out in the sun
Out in the distance
Until it touches your feet
Guarantees me some sort of
Eternal life.

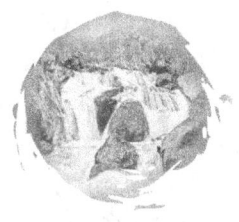

DEFINING PEOPLE

Defining moments?
I scoffed.
They all talked about
Defining moments
But nobody talked about
Defining people.
What about defining people?
They were capable of
Making you quit a maddening job
You hate
Or binge-drink your way
Through the week
They are the ones
That make us half-ourselves
Half-others
Half-here, half-away
They are the ones
That shake the rubble of our soul
Until it leaks

VITALITY

>And to have
>Or have not met
>A few of them
>Is generally what makes
>Or breaks
>A man's life.

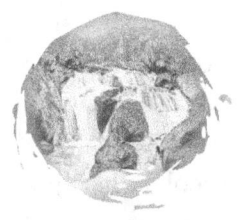

IT TAKES A FEW WORDS

How does it feel
To have something
Holding you off
At the edge
Like a knife slowly turning
Twisting your heart's insides?
How does it feel
To have a few words bouncing
At the tip of your tongue
Like a revolver placed
At the back of your head
With the trigger suspended
Ready to pull
At any moment?
Look at her
Look at her go
Look at her drive

VITALITY

Look at her sing
Look at her dance
Look at her happiness
I look at her
I look at her light
And I wrap myself in darkness
A cold cold blanket
A dark sheet
Keeping me away
From her.
It takes a few words –
It only takes a few words
To bring down walls
To destroy cathedrals
To demolish citadels
It also takes a few words
To instill silence
To draw a continent between two beings
To have to say goodbye
To those sparkling eyes
Waving me off into eternal darkness
Unfair world
Tonight I wish to hold her in my arms
Wherever she is
And whisper into her ear –
I don't care who loves you
And I don't care
If another man ever looks at you again –

Tonight you are mine
Tonight you will doze off to the lullaby of the spheres
And to be able to contemplate that possibility
For me
Means that if all else fails
I am still
A winner.

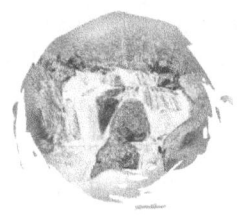

These words are a book

I write to stay sane —
I write to escape from
The job
The hours
The meetings
The deadlines
And the screams.
I write pages and pages
Reams upon reams of words
And I discover that these pages
Are smeared with love.
Now
These words are a book
And now
This book
Is you.

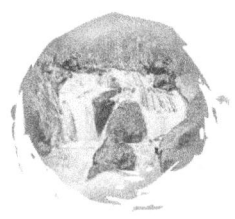

Rules

She is the delicate flower
That cannot be swept away
By the wind

She is the focal point
That makes the job bearable
That makes others bearable
That makes life bearable

Darling,
Tonight my mind is free
My thoughts are unchained
And I can write
The clearest lines:
I would break
All my rules
For you.

VITALITY

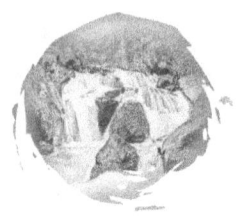

STAGE NAME

I write with my stage name
This poem is an act
Its verses are scripted
And I am the hero of my own play

Tonight I am deviating from the script
Tonight I am tearing down the fourth wall
And bleeding all my failures
In love

And if every failure
Edges me closer to you
Then I invite more of them

You are the link
That ties everything
Together
And I've gone through this feeling
Enough times
To know not to let it slip;

It is the poor man's luck
And the shine
On every rich man's forehead.

And if a time ever comes
When I can lay my head on the pillow
And awaken
Knowing you are mine
Then I would've made it
And the world
Wouldn't owe me a thing.

VITALITY

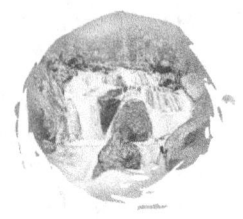

IF SHE READS THIS

If she reads this
I'd want her to know
That I still replay that night
In my head:
That night when
The poor fool in me
Watched her eat 3 pieces
Of pizza in that dimly-lit
Bar.
She ate with grace;
She could even render
The act of eating
A thing of beauty
And grace
And put to shame
Anyone who's ever
Committed it.
And when the barman signaled
To our empty table

I got up
And grabbed
Everything in my
Possession:
My jacket
My wallet
And my beer

I took out the few bills
In my wallet and paid
The man
While she finished her last bite
And rushed after me.
After that
All I could draw from her
Was an angry look
Of disappointment
And regret;
Maybe it was
That damned soul of mine
Acting up again – waging
Mediocre acts of chivalry
To compensate for the words
I couldn't say;
And maybe it was simply me
Throwing away the bills I had
Without bothering to consult the man
For change;
In all cases

VITALITY

I saw the estranged eyes of a girl
I had brought down my walls for
Entirely;
And in retrospect
I would've still defied her
And offered her more
If I could –
The only thing
I would keep
From her
Would be the bottle
Of beer
The bottle where I trapped
All my darkness.
I would like to keep that bottle
Away from her
As much as I can
Because she breathed life
In everything around her;
And to taint
Her vibrancy
With darkness
Would be worse
Than a war crime.
I would have liked
To release the bottle
That night
To get rid of it

And set the darkness free.
But I've brought it back
With me
And now it sits
Over my shoulder
As I write this.

I would also like her
To know
That it was never my intention
To upset her
The slightest;
And now that I write this
I would like her to forgive me
For my foolish mistakes
Mistakes I withdraw
Much like her eyes
Withdraw and shy away
When she is nervous
Or playful.

There is a faucet
Shut tight within me
Brimming with vibrant waves
And a flow of sparkling water
That runs like the river

A faucet waiting to be unplugged
And opened
To release the flow of words

Vitality

From their deep container
To overwhelm the dam
Between me and her

But maybe that's best left
For another poem
Another night

If she reads this.

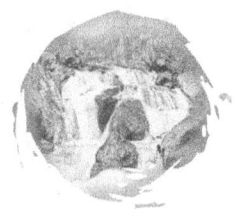

TURNS

And we can take turns
And talk about our own ideas
Of how perfect lovers should be
And how they should shelter each other
From thunderstorms
And you can describe your ideal man
In length
In length
And I can stare at you endlessly
Until you finish
And my only response –
I will borrow
The lines
Of the greats
If I have to
To get my point across –
This
And only this
Shall always stand

VITALITY

And remain valid:
No matter
Where our hearts lie
I am yours
And you
Are
Mine.

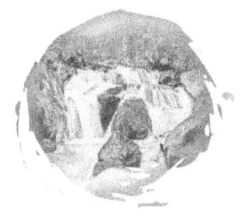

IMPLOSION

All things
Become
All the more
Sweeter
With one element:

A drop of whiskey
At the bottom
Of the cup

The first butterfly
To show up
In spring

Or a kiss from you
On the forehead
Before you take off
With another man?

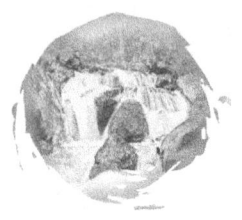

I FIND IT INSANE

I find it insane
That poets trapped in dungeons
Grin about the best lines
Addressed to the finest women
Who will never read them –

But I can believe
Running barefoot
On the grass with you
Or quitting the job
And leaving the money behind
To catch the first plane
And follow you to the other side of the world

Or simply
Sit with you
In a place
We will one day call
Our own that is the dream.

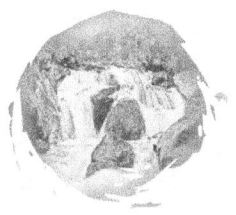

THE ROAD TO YOU

If all my failings
Lead to you
Then I don't mind failing –
I welcome it.
I welcome the treacherous whores
I welcome the revolving door
Of women
Coming in and out of my life
Leaving traces of themselves
On my hardwood floor
I welcome the music in your voice
Whenever you hum along with the radio
I welcome the pounding of our feet
Against the car floor
While we cruise into the open arms of the city
Bathing under city lights
I welcome the strangers you fall in love with
In airports or random cab rides
I welcome the letters addressed to you

VITALITY

Tucked under my sheets
I welcome the dry days
Of emptiness
The lonely nights
Filled with crippling silences and blinding moonlights
I welcome the strength I muster
To say your name –
I welcome the strength I muster
To whisper your name
When you place your head
On my shoulder.

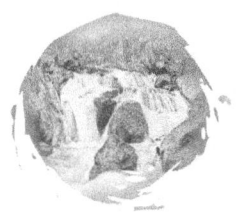

POETIC REASONING

Let them make mistakes.
Let them learn from them.
The poet is a voice for the voiceless
And he is the first one out there
Putting his foot on the line
Touching all the blind spots
Finding them
So that others may cross the bridge
Unmoved
Unshaken.

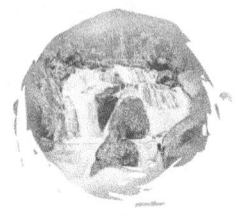

I MADE A DEAL WITH GOD

I made a deal with god
That if I were ever to stand on the edge
Of the world
I would want her
By my side.
'Why her',
He asked.
Because
She has seen
The worst
In me:
The drinking
The fighting
The gambling
The writing
I know it's a little
Played out

And clichéd
But if she put up
With the worst
Then imagine how she
Would handle me
At my best.
'But you are completely
D e t a c h e d
From this girl',
He said.
'This is a girl
You have never held
Or written about
Or serenaded
Or even reminisced about
During your lowly nights
You've only stared at her
From a distance
And loved her
From afar'.
Hey,
I said,
Some of
The best things
Are loved
That way.

VITALITY

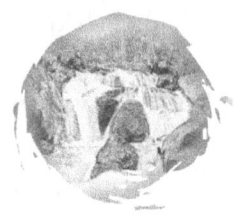

READ THESE LINES

I held her in my arms
And said,
Read these lines.
Is this some kind of trick?
No tricks,
I said.
She read them.
Well,
What do you think?
They're good,
But I still hate poetry.

She was the only one
Who could make all the walls around me
Fall at once
And still make me feel good
About it.

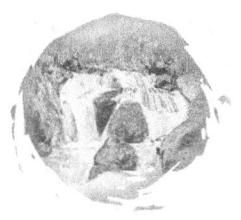

THE DEVILS ARE HERE

The devils are here
The devils are
Here –
We are reminded
That we should look within
To find beauty
But they have already uprooted that garden
The soul is a mess
The human body is a mess
The mind is a poisonous swamp
Filled with swimming blood-thirsty
Alligators

The devils are here
They fly around like little bats
In swarms
Filling up caves and households

VITALITY

Nesting on rooftops
Grazing the city skies

They are born every time
A poet sheds a drop of ink
On paper
They are born every time
A lover's hand is released
They are born every time
A mother picks up the decaying pieces
Of her son's body
They are born
Every time a country martyrs its free-thinkers
To cleanse the hands of its grunts

The devils are here
They are released
in every breath we take
in every word we speak
in every blink of an eye

They are the foot of the ladder
And we are made to climb
Down the shaking steps

The devils are here
They are the tilting vibes
Disrupting our thoughts
Cutting off the currents of our sleep

And on restless nights
They are the dream
That keeps us from dreaming
An escape
They are the maddening hell
That paves itself in our streets
Planting thorns over our seeds

The devils are here
And you can hear them
In the intermittent breaths of forgotten hospital beds
And you can hear them
In the buried weeping of damned graveyards.

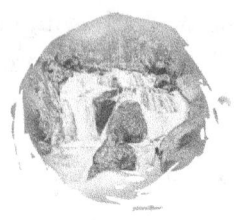

NUMBERS

Overpowered by the sadness
That everything is numbered
Our days are numbered
Our words are numbered
Our lives are numbered
Our breaths are numbered
Our footsteps are numbered
Even our heartbeats
Are numbered…
Look at what we created
The skyscrapers
The machines
The base stations
The city roads
The country fences

Look at the things
The human hand hasn't touched
The free-roaming birds

The morning dew
The rainforests

We don't need control
In order to find freedom
We don't need to keep pushing back
Against the things that were passed down to us

No matter how silly or easy
Or childish it seems

The simplicity of what is around us
Is something to cherish and appreciate
Yet in our minds it is an unfathomable concept
That human beings are only born to maintain
Instead of ravage and turn over
The soils under our feet –
Once pure –
Are now desecrated by our own footprints

There is an instance in us
Begging to let go
Of all things human
And reverse-engineer our thoughts
Revert to its natural state
And until we let it
We will never truly know
What it is to really inhabit
This earth.

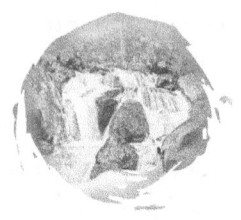

STOP

Slowly
I watch their fire burn down
And run out

Sitting in their offices
Each one of them
Stirring a coffee mug
Looking into it
Observing its sides

It was like looking through
One of Poe's bleak windows
With ravens guarding the sides

They take no joy in their work;
They frustrate themselves over their work
Yet they still exhibit the same swagger
They once did
The first time while walking in these hallways

And the fluorescent lights above their heads
Shine on
Tirelessly
While the bodies beneath them
Slide from the black-coated chairs
Slowly

Slowly they tire
Slowly their minds shift onto better pleasantries
Than the morning news stories shared at work
Slowly their bodies gear towards
Better pastimes
Than taking on endless tasks
Relentlessly
Slowly their faces rebel against
The money-makers
The pocket-fillers
Keeping them alive

But they don't want to be alive
No, they are like the wounded lover
Walking away from the game entirely
Instead of moving on to the next woman
Instead of putting aside one elusive heart
And going after another...
Now one of them has finally surrendered
And broken free from the cycle
A poor devil that chooses to walk home
To escape the car smell of smoked cigars

VITALITY

Amid conference calls organized in traffic
He walks past the markets and notices them
He notices the shoe stores
The cafes

In his apartment he turns on the radio
And, pouring a bourbon,
He hears the music again

The fuckers,
He says,
The fuckers thought they had me
They had me good
But now
Now I have them by the throat

He undoes the tie
Wrapped around his neck
Loosens his shirt
Unbuttons his pants
And drinks
To the light tapping of his feet
Against the soft sounds of the radio.

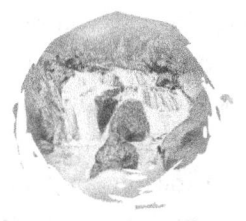

MADNESS

Maybe it was the way
You talked to me –
Sparsely and briefly –
The way your voice popped up
And broke the silence shrouding me

Maybe it was the way
You remembered me on some trivial holiday
That suddenly gained significance
Holidays I now register on my calendar
And remind myself of
Every year

Maybe it was the way you laughed
That silly little laugh
A little girl's laugh I liked to think of it
Like a child smelling a rose for the first time
Or blowing a dandelion
And watching it scatter into pieces in the wind

VITALITY

Maybe it was the way you read my books
And the hidden meanings you uncovered in them
Maybe it was your interpretations
Of my writing
The admiration you had for it
The anticipation you built in me
To write even more

Well now
Now
I look into the cracked ceiling
And I am certain of this:
The silence is gone
And has been replaced
By the humming of your voice
Singing sweet oldies playing on the car radio

The trivial holidays
Still come and go
But I can remember their dates now
And I am able to keep myself sober
Through almost every one of them

The roses in the vase on my coffee table
Have faded
Their petals are weak
But the scent is there
It is faint
But it is still there

And it occasionally fills
The room

And the books
The books are still piled on my desks
Stacked on my shelves
Lined up in the corridor
They are filled with lines
And lines of madness
Obscure profanities
That only come out of jail cells
And escape from madhouses
Pipe leaks that cannot be clogged
Dripping on the head of a prisoner
Bound to a chair in a dungeon

And that madness
Can be traced back to one source:
A single
Human heart
That has forgotten to sing
To another.

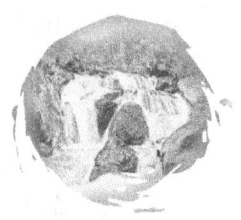

TRACES

Lately everything has stopped:
The peace has stopped
The negotiations have stopped
The massacres have stopped
The riots have stopped
The protests haven't stopped
But they aren't as loud
As they used to be…
Even the writing
Has stopped
The voice in my head
Has stopped
But it still comes back
Every once in a while
And points at you…
The clenching of the heart
Is still there
It hasn't stopped
And your pictures

Your pictures haven't stopped showing up
In my drawers

Your handwriting hasn't stopped
Showing up
On scattered sheets of paper
Left outside on the porch
Abandoned on the couch
Or under some finished bottle
Of beer
Your handwriting that is capable
Of waging war
Of producing walkouts
And shutting down factories
Your name hasn't stopped showing
And the counter
From the last time I uttered it on my lips
Hasn't stopped counting…
The moments haven't stopped
They keep coming back
They won't leave me
These incessant poisonous darts
Needles coming out of the walls
And closing in on me
Moments of ineptitude
Moments of inhibition
That take away everything:
The clothes
The books

Vitality

The writing
The table set

The window panes need refurbishing
From my scratches fighting the thought of you
Fighting to preserve you
Fighting to keep parts of you
Submitting to the moments
That won't stop
That take away everything
As long as they keep
Traces of you.

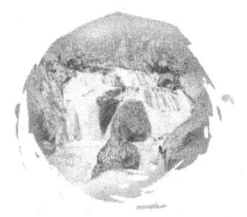

IN ANY ACT OF CREATION

In any act of creation
There is a part
That is inevitably lost
And left out
Like a stain
Between the bedsheets
That has not been removed
Like the small space
On the side of the bed
That is left untouched

In any act of creation
There is a small part of the self
That wanders away
That prolongs its state of fugue
And forgets

VITALITY

Forgets
F o r g e t s …

In any act of creation
There is a piece of talent
That is left buried
In the trenches
A canvas that has been hoaxed
Disfigured
Dismembered
Cursed
And placed among the ruins

In any act of creation
There is some sensibility
That is dropped
In favor of patriotic gunshots
Recognition
And names in big letters
Written on giant billboards

In any act of creation
Quality is invariably
Traded for quantity
And mass production
And chain selling
And marketing

Hanna Abi Akl

In any act of creation
The creator sets foot in the puddle he created
And eventually drowns
In it.

VITALITY

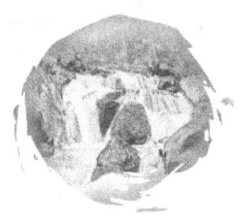

As simply as I can

As simply as I can
I will try to put it
As simply as I can:
You are light
That life cannot
Part with;
You are a necessary infection
Science cannot have a cure for;
You are a question
Left unanswered;
A map
With no destination;
A vision
Every model
Falters and falls
In front of;
A failed
Rhetoric;

I will no longer
Ask for you – if these mere
Lines
Are not enough
To reach you
Then maybe
I never will
But beware of this:
When the will
Of the poet is strong
The words come out
Exploding voraciously from his insides;
Beating against every realm of the universe
Every star the galaxies throw at them
They come out like a violent clubbing
Late at night in an unmonitored neighborhood

And now that you have been encased
In them
You are immortal –
There,
I have said
It
You are
Immortal
Now
And
Forever
And after that

VITALITY

> Darling,
> I guess
> Nothing else
> Really matters
> Anymore.

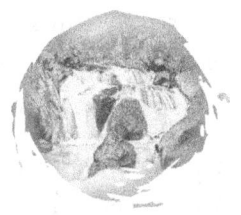

STILL

Still
I find myself writing about you
Your presence breathing down my neck
Your absence a few stop-gaps to exhale
And pull my head out of the vacuum

Still
I find myself writing about you
Every word you speak
Is just another poem
To me

Still
I find myself going back to you
To the places you've been
To the faces you no longer see

Still
There is a hole in my heart
There is a clock that does not tell time

VITALITY

Its arrows stunned
By the constant leaps and lunges of my heart

Still
There is another time
Another era where
Perhaps one would've bet on a different ending
Another period where
Perhaps we would've made it
Together
Another time where
Perhaps I would've escorted you
Down the long stairwell
Into the private low-key dance
Where adults go back to being teenagers
For a night

Still
I look at fireworks
Soaring and blazing through the skies
Popping into different shapes and colors
Drawing faces and lines out of
Hollywood screenplay

Still
I hear faraway show-business girls
Dancing away
In the circus

Still
I read movie lines
And quotes out of literary masterpieces
And insert your name between them

Still
Time stands still
Life stands still
And while you are not here
I am nothing
But the footnote of the page
Trying to elevate myself
And make it back to the top
I am nothing
But the pit of the bottle
The sand tomb in the desert
The lost ship battling the storm
The small fish engulfed by the high tide

Still
I look for your French accent
In a Parisian street
And the smell of baguettes and French cuisine
Takes me back to another time where
I could be writing stories about you
And me
About the way we made it
And forced our way against this life
Sitting pretty on top of the Eiffel tower

VITALITY

    Our legs dangling from the edge
      Our spirits hanging high
        High above the streets
        High above the people
          High above life

          And the shores
          And the operas
       And the printing presses
           And the birds
         And the minefields
          And the streams
        And the traffic lights
         Would stand still.

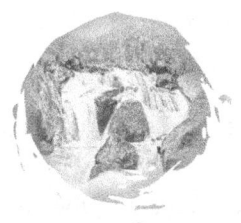

Venture by the Sea

You painted your heart
with sand
And I painted mine
With worn-out whiskey
That I drank and spat out
Countless times

Fleeting –
These are fleeting moments
We have shared
And it makes one wonder if there really is
Such a thing as this strange notion of time
Reigning over us like a tyrannical governor

For only yesterday I sat facing the typer
With my first drink in hand
And today I hold what's left of your heart

Vitality

The pieces erased in the sand
While you go off into the big world

But the waves tell me otherwise
Love,
The waves retrace your footsteps
And mine
To the place where we had never dared venture
To the place where we were
Meant to be.

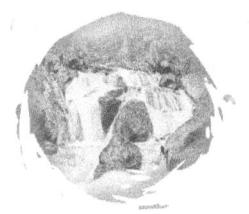

Passing in front of the small humble place

Today
Passing in front of the small humble place
Where we had our first shakes together
I breathe in the sweet sugary aromas
We used to communicate –
They
Like music
Like poetry
Were our medium
Just another channel for us
To talk

Tonight however
I sit on my side of the world
On top of my lonely pillar
Watching her speak to me in words
For the first time in a long while

Vitality

> And I'd like to tell her
> It's good to hear from you.

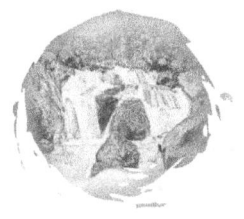

BACKDOOR

Words leave
Backdoors
Behind them
A small trail
To follow
Into a deep dungeon
Or a soft heart.
It's where the unpronounced
Sentiments
Resonate
At equal frequencies;
Where lost lovers' names
Are mapped in the faint ripples
Of the stream;
It is the only place
Where behemoths are taken down
By Davids
And you can still hear the children
Riding their bicycles down the lane.

VITALITY

Words leave
Backdoors
Behind them
And you didn't have to be
A poet
To have one:
The office boy
Or the maintenance guy
Have their own.
It is the only space
Where you can crawl at night
And fit in with them
Or even find in a dark corner
An amateur playing the soft strings of his guitar
Composing a song to his foreign muse
He will likely never sing.

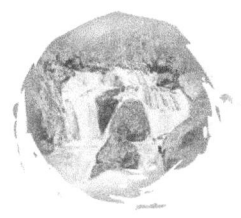

PIPE DREAM

In this creative space
I am surrounded by people
Who convince themselves
They are like me.
They are not.
They are insecure
Trying to mask their weaknesses
In art
While I am a made man
A man on a mission
Chasing a prophecy
Many consider speculation.
No,
This is not a pipe dream
This is the making of
Something special
That will run through the ages
And bridge the fine line
Between time and memory.

VITALITY

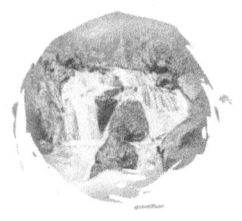

PLACES

I said:
'Baby,
I got places to be
And people to see'
'Then why don't you smile
Like the rest of the people',
She said
'Because some of the most honest
Human beings
Never do.'

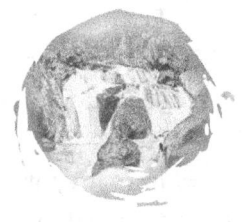

LIGHT-BRINGER

He shuts off the alarm
On his phone
And drags himself
Out of bed:

Another day
At the job
At dealing with
Unfaithful customers
At paying the parking fees
At coming back home
To the constant yelling
That the power's out
At eating heated food
At running into the fat neighbor
At sleeping on the old mattress
Again.

VITALITY

Friend,
We often forget
What it means to make it:
Making it
Comes in many forms
It is a situational victory
That we mistakenly contend with
Instead of celebrating;
In the eyes of those
Who put us out there
We are the trail-blazers
And in our eyes
They are the light-bringers

Friend,
As I sit here
And contemplate
The phone
Waiting for the looming alarm
To kick-start another march
To trigger another daily movement of the masses
I think about her:
She is both here
And not here
Her insisting eyes
Are the reason a thousand paintings are framed
In our museum walls
She has kept me going

Through these small victories
I can now call my own

She is
My light-bringer.

VITALITY

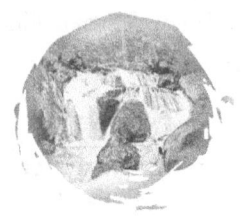

Wonder

It baffles me
That with all the wonder
In the world
So few people
Are in a hurry
To write.

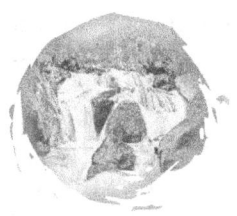

RUBBLE

I hope to see you again
I hope to channel my innermost passions
And have them circulate in your veins
I hope to shake your foundations
To share with you the numbness of my cold hands
When you are absent
I wish to go back in time
And foresee the last time I held you
And turn it into eternity.
The wise don't always win,
Love:
Sometimes they see disaster coming
And still endure it
And write about it later
But it washes away everything
All the same.
To me your portrait is legendary;
A masterpiece forever engraved and recreated
In the history books

VITALITY

Like the great battles
And wars they speak of.
They will speak of you too
One day
Whether I am with you or not
And if I leave this earth
And you happen to find my remains
Know that they are made to worship
What is left of you.
Do not dissolve like ice cubes
Left out in the sun;
Do not make like the quicksand
That pulls away and shrinks
In the absence of movement;
Do not flutter away like the bird
That has tasted freedom
And most importantly
Do not get carried off by the blowing wind
Into the hungry mouths of desperate
Nocturnal fiends
That bite at anything that comes their way.
There is an end
There is an end
And the end is not escape
And if I knew then
What I know now
This entire structure
Would come crumbling down

And you would emerge
And dust off the remains
From the rubble.

VITALITY

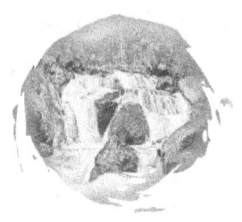

REVIVAL

Maybe Neruda said it best
But I do not love you
Because I love you.
It is my comfort
And my suffering;
To be both the autumn tree
That rots in the cold winter storm
And bears fruit in spring;
To be the winning lottery ticket
On a highway to hell;
I no longer care
About being loved or unloved
I do not seek any kind
Of acceptance;
Your eyes are validation
And rejection;
Your lips a sickness
I haven't quite fully caught;
And your hands – the hands

That ring around me in a garden of colorful
leaves
Are a guilty pleasure
For me to enjoy.
I have lived and not lived
I have beaten death to the finish
I am the finisher
Who delivers the final blow
And lays his opponents to waste.
But if you take such solace in my words
Then know this:
You were my demise
And now
You are
My revival.

VITALITY

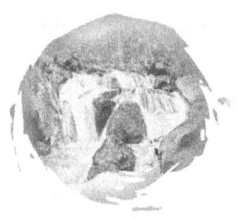

PASSION ON PAPER

I would be lying
If I said I didn't see
The dead;
I walk among them
In school hallways
In dirty parks
In abandoned playgrounds
In rusty hospitals
And noisy junkyards
They walk
And I follow them.
I see the dead
Everywhere
They cause uproars
In usually quiet neighborhoods
They disturb the peaceful homes
Where the elderly snack and sleep
And take slow walks
On the street leading to the city roundabout

Hanna Abi Akl

They walk
And I walk with them.
They walk into the graveyards
Trash the art galleries
The theaters
And disrupt the nightly news
They walk
And I walk in front of them.
What is left of me
Is not blood or bones or skin
It's fear;
Fear of what was
Fear of what is to come
How did I get here
And where I should go
From here
Are two concurrent questions
My mind will never answer
But the only thing left pouring out of me
Is the sinister specter of these words
Shadowing my ice-cold veins
The same veins that are distributed onto every home at night
After the children have been put to bed
I walk
I walk past the living
I walk past the dead
I walk past the graveyards

VITALITY

Past the funeral homes
Past the confession chambers
Past the gates of heaven
I walk.
And the dim light that is always on
Past midnight
In a small one-bedroom apartment house
Is my own;
I write
To stay clear from the dead
I write
To escape their faces
And though the horizon is cloudy
And full of uncertainties
I can discern
The only living thing
In sight:
Your face
Standing atop of a pile of dead bodies
Walking on the sea of the dead
I recognize the glow from your flower dress
Shining on
Shining on in a rare ray of light
That comes upon me in the form of simple words
I spent a lifetime searching for:
Your presence
Is
My salvation.

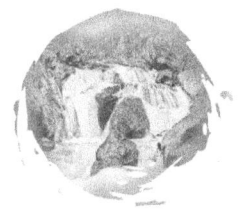

TOAST

Here's to the madness
We add
To our undertakings

Here's to the revolutions
We vouch for
Against anarchy

Here's to the dreams
We strive to always keep viable
In a world of impossibilities

And above all
Here's to bringing the ones we love
A little closer to us
Each day.

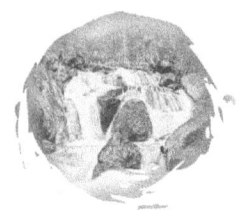

A LIGHT

All it takes
Is a light
To show us the way

All it takes
Is a light
To ignite the flame

All it takes
Is a light
To start the spark

We must never fall
Into dank submission
But believe
That light
Constitutes
The very essence
Of our being.

I LENT HER MY HEART

I lent her my heart
She lent me the ocean
I lent her my soul
She lent me the wind
I lent her my words
She lent me her voice

All the poetry books
In the world
Cannot cover your name

All the magic
In the universe
Cannot contain your eyes

And the dark souls you have faced
The demons you have come up against
And slain

Are now crawling toward the tree of life
Bearing your fruit –
The fruit of survival

Darling,
I don't take pride in my asking
But I take pride in my surrender
And while I dance with the nightingales
The bats swarm above my head
Screeching
Screeching
The viper slithers toward my feet
And a statue of clay
Made out of your naked body
Carries the flag of my poor country

Where is your heart?
What are your dreams?
Do you still carry around
Your little box
Full of darkness?

Let the poor man share your darkness
Let the poor man share your bread
Let the devils laugh at my disfigured face
Placed on the side of your left breast
My lips licking yours
My arms holding your hips together

And the words
The words coming out of me
Forever etching your name
Across the borderline of my forgotten country.

VITALITY

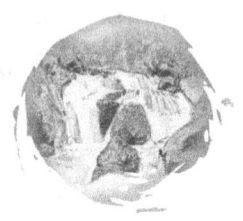

WE FORGET TO FEEL

The problem
With today's writers
Is that they tell stories;
They don't write
Sadness
They don't paint
Passion
They don't spread
Absence in their words.
Love,
Tonight I watch you paint
Paint your soul with words
Draw an ocean covered by a white skyline
And I prepare the bed of roses
The red sheets that will shelter us both
From all harm and destruction

Hanna Abi Akl

Love,
We get so lost
In art
And words
And life
That sometimes
We forget to feel

We forget terribly
The aches of the soul
And trade them for the safety of the mind
But the soul was never made for the net
It was made for the ocean
The high tides pushing and pulling against
The frame in the wall
And I can see the water dripping
And splattering on the floor
All the way to the rose bed

Love,
Tonight I prepare my final prayer
I ask the word god to be good to me one more time
To bless my words
To bless the brush in my hand
To bless the red sheets again…

Tonight I will forget the words
And soak myself in whatever is left of
My defunct soul

VITALITY

And worship
Worship the woman that started the change
Worship the woman that restored every
Sense of inspiration
Worship the white dove of love

Love,
Tonight I come to you with a single request:
Don't
forget
To
feel

And when your soul awakens
I will be there waiting
By the rose bed.

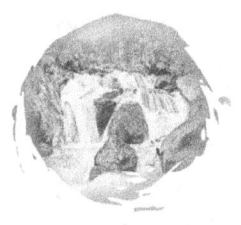

BREATHING YOU

In front of you is standing a naked man
In front of you is standing a naked man
Breathing you
Breathing every inch of you
But you clutch and you withdraw
And you close and you shut out tightly
Clinching your entire body
Wrapping your soft silky skin around a pole
You pull away
And then you open up again
For brief instants
Like a blossoming flower that has survived the winter
Just barely blooming at the beginning of spring…
In front of you is standing a naked man
But you refuse the shattered pieces
You refuse the touch
You refuse the flirty looks
You refuse the words
You shut your ears and refuse the music

VITALITY

You refuse the words...
And the music drowns
The noise is drowned out
The words fade and the lasting marks of ink
Slowly disappear
Erased from paper and memory
The blinds come down over the windows
And the light vanishes
But the man remains...
In front of you is standing a naked man
Wearing your body
Wearing your mind
Curling up in the palm of your hands
Still following you with his enchanted eyes
That refuse to go away...
In front of you is standing a naked man
A man that has made it through the rain
Survived the pits of hell
The flames of inferno
The terrible dust and turbulent sandstorm

And what do you see...
You see a reflection of your soul
You see an embrace
You thought you would never
Know.

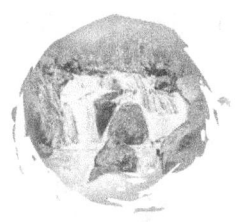

LUCK OF THE WORD

They still worry
About their little jobs
When we have countries
Waiting at our gates
To devour us
Street urchins that are prepared
To go to war
They still worry about their money
The small bumps in their cars
Their wives, their girlfriends
The women they desperately want to impress
But can't talk to
And where is the word
In all of this?
What is its place?
What of the luck of the word?
It will not save you.
It will not save me.
It will not save us.

VITALITY

Yet I am still here
Writing
Trying to send it
Forcing my tired fingers
To get it out
And they ask me
What of it
What of it all
Well darlings
This is the only reason
I haven't allowed my mind
To wander to those narrow streets
Of darkness and triviality.

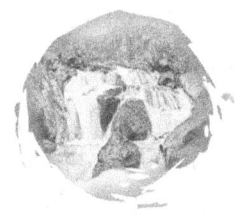

Mockingbird

Between you and me
Are majestic cathedrals
Gothic walls
Tainted with suburban art
Evening beers shared outside
In the cold streaming European winds
A great blazing Mediterranean sun

Between you and me
Are scattered pieces
On my hardwood floor
Little letters
I was never able to send
Soundtracks registered
And replayed in my old car

Between you and me
There is a freezing ocean
There is an underwater island

VITALITY

There is a flock of seagulls
Headed for the harbor

Between you and me
There is the homeless
There is the penniless
There is the worthless

Between me and you
There is the punching machine
There is the coffee table
There is a continent

And still at night from your window
You will hear the tender beating of this fragile heart

Now,
This is not a poem in the palm of my hands
This is a
Mockingbird.

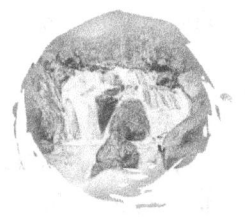

SALVATION

It doesn't take much for me
To wander away from my most insecure thoughts
And it doesn't take me much
To come back to them;
And with you away
They are one word
They are two syllables
They are your name

And with you away
There is an emptiness
An entire nation
Cannot fill;
And with you away
There is an emptiness
A library of books cannot fill;
And with you away
There is a silence

Vitality

The radio music
Cannot fill;

You are the music
You are the library of books
You are the nation of quiet people
Moving steadfast
Angry and oppressed
Sad and forbidden
From crossing over to the land of wealth;
You are the habits I keep drowning into
The faltering thoughts that cripple me
And partition my mind

You are the soul-splitting ache
Left by your absence
And until you return
There is a void
Looming over us all
A constant vortex looking to sweep us off our feet
And we wait for it

We wait for the shades of grey and black
To take over this comical stage
We wait for your name
To be called out of the skies again
We wait for your footsteps
To retrace their way from the sun
Back to this unholy earth

And I fall back
Into my habits
I fall back easily
Into my dark cocoon
And the insecure thoughts
Panting, panting
My way, my way
Are renditions of your name
And your presence
Is my
Salvation.

VITALITY

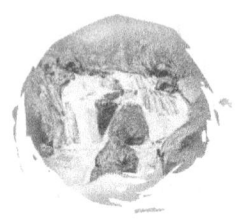

WORLD VIEW

Forcefully;
I am sometimes prone
To looking at things
Forcefully;
The way the world moves
The way it is made to reshape our thoughts
And control our vision
Like a stone mountain
Rising from the earth's core
I peek through the keyhole of the world
And see
That our bodies
Are hollow
And see-through;
That it is not blood
But spirit water
That courses through our veins;
That skylines
Are mere drawings

In a children's playbook;
That the last bit
Of sanity
Has been spared and saved
By the human race;
That artwork
Has attracted more followers
Than machine guns;
This and less of this
This and more of this
This
And
You;
That whether you are here
Or away
You aren't always
At the forefront on my lines.

VITALITY

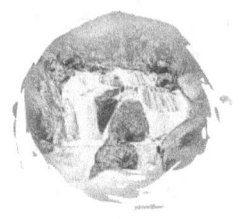

DONT GO LOOKING FOR HEROES

There are no superheroes
In this part of the world
Only mercenaries
Who've held their breaths
For so long;
Some of them
Have forgotten
To breathe
And the only thought
That eludes them
Is seeking shelter
From every imminent quake.

They hold on to their roots
They hold on to their native land
Their language
Their recipes
Their form of dialogue

But those are not enough
To make them last:
They do not render them
Any more memorable.

There are no superheroes here
There are no superheroes
In this corner of the world
Only fighter planes
Circling dark skies
Blighting defenseless youth
Forcing unprepared men and women
To go to war
And burying lives
Under piles of rubble.

There are no superheroes here
There are no gods
To reach out to
Only few men of words
And action
Walking inside dark tunnels
Exhaling their last breaths
In small echoless voices
That lead nowhere.

VITALITY

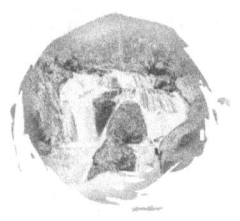

STILL-FRAME

My favorite picture
Will always be
The still-frame image of us
Sitting and talking
About meaningless subjects
Constantly reinventing each other
Every time our eyes meet;
Whether you are here
Or in some foreign
Faraway land
We could be discussing the snow falling
Or a quote we read somewhere
In some forgotten book
Or even a song that crossed our mind
On that day;
And you would be wearing
Your winter grey sweater
And the necklace holding a singular pearl

That big white orb hanging from it
Shining around your neck

There is a weakness in love
A magnificent weakness
That overshadows the individualistic strengths
That make up its center

The still-image of us reappears in my thoughts
And in my confession to the gods
I would like nothing more
Than to caress your forbidden black hair
Flowing in every direction of the wind
But I am restrained;
Yes darling
I am restrained by the chains of love
And obligation and duty
And all else that gets in the way of me and you

It is a sin –
I wish to think it is a sin
To get in the way of pure love
And not allow it to take its final form

And I would like nothing more
Than to fall on the pillow tonight
Knowing I have finally broken free
Of the constraints:

VITALITY

>Loving you
Was more than a simple victory
It was a triumph
For all mankind
And tonight
I know
I am
Invincible.

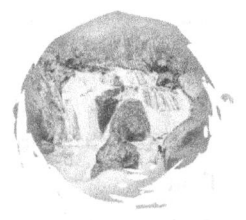

SIGNS OF LOVE

You are never truly loved
By a writer
Unless that love
Is written down
And put to words.
It's a different kind of love;
It's different from
Holding hands
While walking down a lane
Or kissing in public
Or writing small letters
To each other
Using silly nicknames.
It's like going out
On a snowy day
In France
And having a snowball fight
With no clear winner
Or sharing a song

Vitality

No one else really listens to
Or likes
Or painting a portrait
Of your favorite person
That no one else
Can recognize
When held against
The bright light.

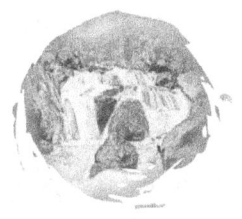

YELLOW FLOWER

In the worst of times
We could still sit
And talk about French philosophy
And she would run her fingers
Along my face
All the way down to my jawline
Looking at me with the eyes
Of someone
Who was slowly constructing the world
Back alone;
Piece by piece
And I would look back
Asking about all the chaos
That surrounded us
And if there ever would be an end
To it
But she would interrupt me –
She would interrupt my thoughts
By lifting her cup

VITALITY

Of hot chocolate
And drinking from it
With grace
Beauty
All the things that were lost
And went missing from this world
She would remind me that
She still possessed them
And that's when I would start to believe
That maybe Sartre and De Beauvoir
And Camus
Had it wrong
Maybe things were taking a turn for the better
And she'd hold my hand
To encourage these thoughts
And present me
A yellow flower
Asking me about that peculiar color
And what it represented.
I think it's a symbol for jealousy,
She'd say.
Whatever it was
On that night
It clearly represented
One thing:
Hope.

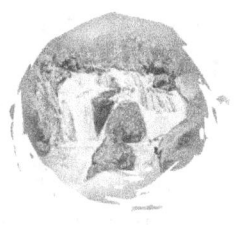

COFFEE LADY

My first mistake was
Asking her out for coffee.
After that
I only remember sipping the dark liquid
From a mug off the bed stand
While we lay in bed together.
She was a good woman –
A good woman who didn't believe she could make it
Like all the good ones did –
She knew her poetry;
She handled her alcohol
Decently.
She was always sharp
Far sharper than me
And I could feel her
Scrutinizing me
Every time
We sat together.
She didn't want to be held

VITALITY

She didn't want anyone
To have to walk her anywhere
Or take her to places;
The world was hers
And every time she sipped her black coffee
She owned another piece of it.

I go back to my books
I go back to my writings
I go back to pictures
Of old
To try and understand
Why good things
Always evade us
So narrowly;
Why the things that seem to bring us joy
Are the ones that ultimately cause our downfall
And why we cling on to them so dearly
Like weak tree branches
Moments before being ripped off
By the heavy storm.

Now a black line of coffee
Is all that separates us;
And she is still a ball of fire
Untamed, uncontrolled, unfiltered
Cruising alone
Riding the high tide
And I wait for her by the corner

Of the coffee shop
That tails a small bookstore
In a forgotten back-alley

And the next time I see her
I will ask her:
Do you want
To go
Out
For
Coffee?

VITALITY

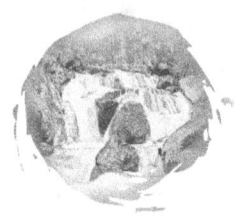

REGRESSION

Here I go again
Boarding the same train
Riding the egotistical one-way ride
A trip to no man's land
A road to death valley.
There is no beyond
There is no aftermath
Just plain old dust
Kicked into the wind
People who are short of breath
Still ejaculating air
Into the closed sky.

I hold a book in my hand
Faded now
From memory
But it is a good book
And like all books

It never leaves
Unless you allow it.

There is a scent in the air
A recognizable smell
Of being here before
Or finding myself here
Before.

A woman
A woman had asked me
To carry this book with me;
A woman
Had asked me
To bring that book
And read some of the lines
Inscribed in it
To her.

Now she is gone
She has boarded another train
And the book is still firmly
Clutched in my hand

The train still goes on
And outside my window I see erased mountain tops
And a black sky covered with grey powder
Swallowing a faded sunset.

VITALITY

I revert
I revert
To my primal state
To my instinctive state of being
Not that of the predator
Or the ragged man
But the state of loneliness
That has cupped me
In its hands
For so long.

It is the road
I have never lost
The small haven I can always return to
The prison that keeps me caged from aggression
And as long as I am
There
The train
Will stride on
With no signs of stopping.

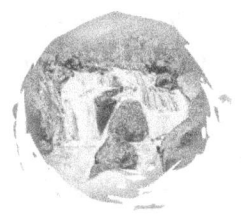

ODE TO THE STORM

Let me tell you
A few things
About writers:
They don't travel
In packs
Like wolves
Rather,
They are like the lone wolf
You always see
Howling atop the mountain
In fancy expensive paintings.

Writers always choose
A subject matter
And stick to it –
And while these seem
Like grandiose ideas
And difficult concepts
They are in truth

VITALITY

Things close to their hearts;
They only speak of
The things they know
And think they understand
Well enough
To explain.

Writers
Are not a force of nature
They are just a breed
Designed to craft and transmit
Their thoughts
Through words.

And tonight
Sitting here by the hot fire
I can feel the cold storm
Taking over your heart.

Forgive me
Forgive me for not being able
To walk through the hurricane
With you
Forgive me
For easily getting lost in the snow
But snow leaves footprints
And i will retrace them
To find my way to you.

Tonight
Don't think of me as a man
Forget that i am a lover
And think of me
As someone
Hiding behind the words
Resorting to the best tools
At my disposal
To say what is in my heart;
For here is another thing
You should know
About writers:

Most of them
Are able to arrange elements in peculiar
Lines to showcase their hidden desires
And put down matter into words until their
Knuckles start to bleed.

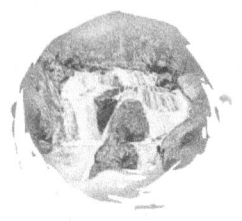

CROSSING OVER TO YOU

Warped back into nothingness
I find myself at the starting line
Again:
We were two pawns
Moving on different chessboards
Pieces that were never meant
To match
Or even be placed opposite
One another
But we created that intersection.
No,
This is not a cry out
To the fatalists
Nor spite aimed toward those who dismiss them
And believe the black cat is not destined
To walk down the lonely aisle
This is a far cry to the stars.

We've moved between dimensions
And somehow ended up here.
Now,
I see your face in dirty coffee mugs
I smell your scent on the clothes I wore around
you
I have flashbacks of you every time I taste food
We've shared together.
This is not an obsession
And this is not coincidental
They say writing chooses the individual
And turns him into a writer
Now tell me dear,
Does love also choose the man
And turn him into a lover?

About the Author

Hanna Abi Akl is a Lebanese-born English writer. He lived in Beirut before moving to France in 2018. Hanna writes contemporary poetry and prose. He has been heavily featured in literary magazines and is a writer and ambassador of Beirut Poetics, the Beirut-based poetry branch of the Poetryhood movement. Hanna has already published his debut novel, A Road Away From Home (2017) as well as his debut poetry collection, Diary In Poems (2018).

www.ingramcontent.com/pod-product-compliance
Lightning Source LLC
Chambersburg PA
CBHW070529010526
44118CB00012B/1080